Complete Hor

Aquarius 2022

Monthly astrological forecasts for 2022

TATIANA BORSCH

Translated from Russian by Sonja Swenson-Khalchenia
Translation copyright © Coinflow Limited, Cyprus
AstraArt Books is an imprint of Coinflow limited, Cyprus
Published by Coinflow Limited, Cyprus
For queries please contact: tatianaborsch@yahoo.com

ISBN: 978-9925-579-76-1 (print)
ISBN: 978-9925-579-77-8 (ebook)

Contents

2022 – A World Still in Flux

We survived the incredible stress of 2020-2021, when our world's very foundation seemed to be falling apart under us. What does 2022 have in store?

According to the stars, the coming year can be divided into two distinct periods: a very favorable time during the first half of the year, and trouble during the second half.

Politics and economy

From January to July, things will be serene and predictable.

Jupiter and Neptune will dominate this period, and nearly all year long, they will have very strong energy in Pisces. Jupiter's contact with other planets, including Uranus and Pluto, will be exceptionally favorable during the first half of 2022, so we can count on calm, steady waters...

Together in Pisces, Jupiter and Neptune rule the areas of medicine, oil, space, and the sea. Their favorable aspects mean that this is where we can expect a lot of developments in 2022. In addition to medicine, oil, and space, Jupiter and Neptune also rule the arts, so we can expect incredible feats in film, music, and painting. Many of these pieces will have a space or maritime theme.

Neptune also rules everything related to drugs and alcohol, and 2022 may bring a trend toward legalizing drugs in many countries. This will mainly include "soft" drugs, such as marijuana. This is also a promising time for the wine industry, and Jupiter's powerful influence means that we might see increasing production, and more public attention on elite, luxury wine brands.

For now, we will still have to deal with problems related to the economy, but during the first half of the year, they will likely be somewhat mitigated and under control. One way or another the world will start to shake off the coronavirus epidemic, with help from vaccines and new, effective treatments.

Many countries, including Russia, the United States, and China, will rebuild their economies, and shift their direction and approach. Here, we can consider China as the unrefuted global leader.

During the first half of the year, we might see cryptocurrencies experience serious growth, along with the emergence of new cryptocurrencies.

Things are looking less sunny for the EU countries. Despite the fact that the interminable lockdowns will finally come to an end, economies will continue to struggle, and political clashes will continue.

However, during the first half of the year, from January until mid-August, these negative trends will be somewhat less noticeable.

Things in the United States are looking much more peaceful, though Republicans will become more powerful and influential in 2022.

During the first half of the year, the political horizon of our turbulent world is looking relatively quiet. There will be a trend toward resalable relationships toward war and peace, and there may even be major agreements between countries, which will be largely responsible for this state of affairs.

Beginning in the second half of August 2022, however, things will suddenly take a dark turn. Confrontation from Mars is the theme of the second half of the year. This will lead to negativity, crises, and war. In May 2022, Jupiter will also shift from neutral Pisces to belligerent Aries.

The international stage will once again become difficult, and many countries will fail to shoulder their agreements, with hotspots popping up all over the globe. This may become extremely challenging, as Uranus, an abrupt planet full of the unexpected, will be in the same degree of Taurus that it was in 1938, which was a fateful year for the entire world.

Remember that 1938 was the year that Germany, Poland, and Romania divided Czechoslovakia with the agreement of England and France. From an astrological point of view, this is the event that triggered World War Two. Of course, astrology is not alone here – when describing the dissolution of Czechoslovakia, Winston Churchill himself stated that "England has been offered a choice between war and shame. She has chosen shame, and will get war."

Uranus has an 84-year cycle. Its passage through Taurus has always brought large-scale war, including in 1853-1856, with the Crimean Wars, between the Russian Empire and a coalition made up of Britain, France, the Ottoman Empire, and Sardinia.

Uranus entered Taurus on May 5, 2018, and will remain there until April 26, 2026. We already know that between 2018 and 2021, military tensions have escalated around the world. Unfortunately, this is only the beginning of what may continue for a long time into the future.

Warmongering rhetoric and possibly even clashes in hotspots will be more common during the second half of the year, but this will result in the weakening of NATO countries, with China and Russia growing stronger. This may continue into 2023-2024.

During this time, many countries will experience spontaneous protests and unrest. People will begin to resist authority much more strongly, which will force authorities to make some concessions and adopt certain measures, as many countries will find themselves moving closer to revolution. Countries suffering from economic instability are likely to see changes in government, if not outright political chaos.

The horoscope for the United States indicates that in the second half of 2022, there will be turbulence as well as the revelation of certain secrets. Former President Donald Trump will take on an active role and should not be written off. His influence on US citizens will only grow, but political positions will in general become more hardline. All of that will go along with a serious struggle and clashes with democratic institutions.

Protests and unrest are to be expected in Russia, too, during this time. However, President Putin will hold onto power, though there may be some changes to various government bodies. The changes that began with changes in government in 2020 may continue. Of course, some people will suffer, but overall, this will be a good thing for society.

The economic and political situation in Ukraine may worsen in the long term. Military activity in the eastern territories of Luhansk and Donetsk will continue, and that may end poorly for Kyiv, and it will become clear that these territories will never be returned to Ukraine.

Problems that arise during the second half of 2022 will continue during the three months of 2023.

Climate

The climate will continue to change. Jupiter and Neptune will bring major floods that are worse than what we have seen in the last several years. People living in coastal areas should consider this and take the utmost precautions when preparing for spring. Volcanos will also become more active. Glaciers will continue melting, and there is nothing we can do to halt this process.

In late May, Jupiter will move into fiery Aries, and remain there until the end of October. This means that during this time, we can expect fires to break out around the world, causing major ecological and human losses.

In seismically active zones, we can expect major earthquakes.

Health

In 2022, we may see new, unique treatments for serious illnesses such as diabetes and cancer.

From May to November, people should be very careful if they suffer from heart disease or various allergies. In the fall and winter of 2022, we might see new outbreaks of respiratory infections.

During the second half of 2022, we might also see the emergence of new types of diseases. We may also learn new information about the manmade origins of coronavirus, which dominated our world in 2020 and 2021.

Personal life

The first half of 2022 is a good time for buying real estate or opening up a business.

Single people might meet someone special, and Pisces, those born in the first ten days of Aries, as well as Virgo and Capricorn will be ahead of the rest of the planet in this regard.

Any marriages that take place between January and May are sure to be stable and happy.

Children born in 2022 might grow up to be talented musicians, highly creative, and have extrasensory abilities. In time, they will become inspiring leaders who will steer the world to a positive place.

During the fall and winter of 2022, things will be rocker in politics as well as personal relations. Many people will reconsider their links to others, and a real crisis or breakdown is likely.

If that is your case, remember that any crisis and break with the past is the key to true change, new opportunities, and a new life! This is the only way we can deal with the twists and turns Fate throws our way!

2022 Overview for Aquarius

Overall, 2022 is a positive year for you. You will have new opportunities in both work and your personal life. However, try to control your emotions and finances as you surrender to the will of Fate.

Work. During the first half of the year, most Aquarians who work will manage to climb the career ladder and seriously improve their resumes. It may not be everything you dreamt of, but in time, you are sure to appreciate its value, as well as your future prospects.

This includes cooperation with people in other cities or abroad. The first glimmers of this will appear during the summer – from late May until August. Things will become more formal in 2023.

In 2022, entrepreneurs can count on lucrative deals, while employees can count on a promotion and salary bump.

In September, however, things will begin to change, and not for the better. Those who depend on contacts with colleagues from afar might face various types of roadblocks – some things will still need to be finalized, or perhaps shifts on the global stage will become a real thorn in your side. Perhaps issues in your personal life will appear and throw a wrench in your plans. Remember, everyone's got problems, so consider your options and act accordingly.

During this time, entrepreneurs will have to invest resources into their projects, and it will end up being more costly than they had anticipated. From September to December, you will face ruin on many fronts, and the things you worked so hard for may simply go up in smoke.

Closer to the end of the year, many Aquarians will have a chance to resolve most of these issues and get things back on track with their colleagues in other cities or abroad.

Money. You will experience a lot of financial ups and downs in 2022. During the first half of the year, you will have more money, but later on, you will have to rely on what you make in late October and November. In September, October, and December, you will face a lot of expenses, either related to work, your personal life, or your family and children's needs.

Love and family. Various areas of your personal life may undergo changes this year.

You may have a summer romance, and you would like to have something beyond just sex and having fun with each other. This may happen on a trip or among people who have come from far away. This fall, however, your relationships may turn sour, for various reasons. In any case, one thing is clear – you can forget about a peaceful, tranquil life.

In December, you will be able to fix everything, so do not make any rash decisions, and just try to get through it. Things may not be so bad, after all, and next year, you will have an opportunity to continue the relationship.

Many couples will be busy dealing with matters related to real estate in 2022, and this is sure to dominate their plans.

Spouses might face problems with their children during the second half of the year. In the best-case scenario, you will have to spend money on their development, studies, or training, and in the worst cases, you will have to resolve their problems for them, and that may take up the lion's share of your family budget.

Many Aquarians will have plans related to a move, and in some cases, that will be to a place where you have previously lived or visited several times before. That will happen in the summer of 2022 at the earliest, and into 2023 at the latest.

Health. In 2022, you are feeling less than spritely, so live a healthy lifestyle and take good care of yourself.

January

New York Time			London Time		
Calendar Day	Lunar Day	Lunar Day Start Time	Calendar Day	Lunar Day	Lunar Day Start Time
01/01/2022	29	6:06 AM	01/01/2022	29	6:42 AM
02/01/2022	30	7:10 AM	02/01/2022	30	7:49 AM
02/01/2022	1	1:35 PM	02/01/2022	1	6:35 PM
03/01/2022	2	8:06 AM	03/01/2022	2	8:42 AM
04/01/2022	3	8:51 AM	04/01/2022	3	9:21 AM
05/01/2022	4	9:29 AM	05/01/2022	4	9:51 AM
06/01/2022	5	10:01 AM	06/01/2022	5	10:15 AM
07/01/2022	6	10:30 AM	07/01/2022	6	10:36 AM
08/01/2022	7	10:56 AM	08/01/2022	7	10:54 AM
09/01/2022	8	11:23 AM	09/01/2022	8	11:12 AM
10/01/2022	9	11:49 AM	10/01/2022	9	11:30 AM
11/01/2022	10	12:18 PM	11/01/2022	10	11:51 AM
12/01/2022	11	12:50 PM	12/01/2022	11	12:15 PM
13/01/2022	12	1:27 PM	13/01/2022	12	12:44 PM
14/01/2022	13	2:08 PM	14/01/2022	13	1:20 PM
15/01/2022	14	2:56 PM	15/01/2022	14	2:05 PM
16/01/2022	15	3:49 PM	16/01/2022	15	2:58 PM
17/01/2022	16	4:46 PM	17/01/2022	16	3:58 PM
18/01/2022	17	5:47 PM	18/01/2022	17	5:05 PM
19/01/2022	18	6:49 PM	19/01/2022	18	6:15 PM
20/01/2022	19	7:52 PM	20/01/2022	19	7:26 PM
21/01/2022	20	8:56 PM	21/01/2022	20	8:38 PM
22/01/2022	21	10:00 PM	22/01/2022	21	9:52 PM
23/01/2022	22	11:06 PM	23/01/2022	22	11:06 PM
25/01/2022	23	12:14 AM	25/01/2022	23	12:23 AM
26/01/2022	24	1:24 AM	26/01/2022	24	1:42 AM
27/01/2022	25	2:35 AM	27/01/2022	25	3:02 AM
28/01/2022	26	3:45 AM	28/01/2022	26	4:19 AM
29/01/2022	27	4:51 AM	29/01/2022	27	5:30 AM
30/01/2022	28	5:50 AM	30/01/2022	28	6:28 AM
31/01/2022	29	6:40 AM	31/01/2022	29	7:13 AM

You can find the description of each lunar day in the chapter "A Guide to The Moon Cycle and Lunar Days"

Luck is on your side – right now, you have incredible potential, and you can channel it as you see fit. Surprise yourself and others!

Work. Most Aquarians are grappling with organizational matters this month. You may have to deal with a property dispute, most likely over real estate, but this is not the first time something like this has arisen. A large part of the challenge will take place during the second half of January, and things will not be resolved until the second half of February. You have the potential to win – most likely in the distant future – slow and steady wins the race. Keep your head down and put your nose to the grindstone.

There might also be new opportunities for you on the horizon this year. You might see the first glimmers in January, but things will be much clearer in March and April.

Money. Your financial situation is stable, with a clear upward trend. In addition to your usual income, this month you can count on support from partners, credit, and even profit from various real estate transactions.

Those who are not part of the business world can count on assistance from parents, your spouse, or a loved one.

Love and family. In many cases, the major events this month will involve your personal life. During the first ten days of January, you might finally get a chance to relax and forget about work for a while. It doesn't matter where – at home, on the couch, on a hammock on a sunny beach, or the countryside – the important thing is getting a chance to relax and get away from it all.

During the last twenty days, you will feel agitated, and you might have to deal with some issues related to your place of residence. That might be repairs, acquiring something new, or redecorating.

In other cases, you may be dealing with a lengthy divorce, difficult negotiations involving joint property or a joint residence.

For couples, January looks neutral. There is nothing new, and that is neither good nor bad.

Health. This month, you are not particularly energetic, so try to give yourself time to relax, especially since January provides you with so many opportunities to do just that.

Take care of elderly members of your family, as they are likely to face various types of problems.

February

New York Time			London Time		
Calendar Day	Lunar Day	Lunar Day Start Time	Calendar Day	Lunar Day	Lunar Day Start Time
01/02/2022	1	12:49 AM	01/02/2022	1	5:49 AM
01/02/2022	2	7:22 AM	01/02/2022	2	7:48 AM
02/02/2022	3	7:57 AM	02/02/2022	3	8:15 AM
03/02/2022	4	8:28 AM	03/02/2022	4	8:38 AM
04/02/2022	5	8:56 AM	04/02/2022	5	8:57 AM
05/02/2022	6	9:23 AM	05/02/2022	6	9:16 AM
06/02/2022	7	9:50 AM	06/02/2022	7	9:35 AM
07/02/2022	8	10:19 AM	07/02/2022	8	9:55 AM
08/02/2022	9	10:50 AM	08/02/2022	9	10:18 AM
09/02/2022	10	11:25 AM	09/02/2022	10	10:45 AM
10/02/2022	11	12:04 PM	10/02/2022	11	11:18 AM
11/02/2022	12	12:50 PM	11/02/2022	12	11:59 AM
12/02/2022	13	1:40 PM	12/02/2022	13	12:49 PM
13/02/2022	14	2:36 PM	13/02/2022	14	1:47 PM
14/02/2022	15	3:36 PM	14/02/2022	15	2:52 PM
15/02/2022	16	4:38 PM	15/02/2022	16	4:01 PM
16/02/2022	17	5:42 PM	16/02/2022	17	5:13 PM
17/02/2022	18	6:47 PM	17/02/2022	18	6:26 PM
18/02/2022	19	7:52 PM	18/02/2022	19	7:40 PM
19/02/2022	20	8:58 PM	19/02/2022	20	8:56 PM
20/02/2022	21	10:06 PM	20/02/2022	21	10:12 PM
21/02/2022	22	11:15 PM	21/02/2022	22	11:31 PM
23/02/2022	23	12:25 AM	23/02/2022	23	12:50 AM
24/02/2022	24	1:34 AM	24/02/2022	24	2:07 AM
25/02/2022	25	2:40 AM	25/02/2022	25	3:18 AM
26/02/2022	26	3:40 AM	26/02/2022	26	4:19 AM
27/02/2022	27	4:31 AM	27/02/2022	27	5:08 AM
28/02/2022	28	5:15 AM	28/02/2022	28	5:45 AM

You can find the description of each lunar day in the chapter "A Guide to The Moon Cycle and Lunar Days"

All month long, you will heroically overcome the obstacles that have been rearing their heads lately. But this time, the circumstances are just right, and you will be able to overcome it all!

Work. Your main task this month will be something very important related to some sort of property, possibly land or real estate. It seems that this time, there is a real desire to resolve a longstanding problem, but there are a few loose ends you need to discuss, first.

Alternatively, you may be trying to expand your business or deal with major construction. This will give you the upper hand, whether you are a manager or entrepreneur. If this is your case, you will have to grapple with a series of organizational tasks, but thanks to your discipline and hardworking nature, you will manage just fine.

Employees can get ready to see some success during the second half of the month or even in March. There is a promotion on the horizon, or possibly some additional responsibilities in your current position. Naturally, all of this goes hand in hand with a raise.

Money. Your financial situation will be stable, with significant improvements this month. In addition to your usual earnings, many Aquarians can also count on large profits from favorable real estate transactions. You might also receive a loan on very favorable terms, or financial support from a business partner. Those who are not part of the business world can count on support from parents or a loved one.

Love and family. Many Aquarians are fully immersed in their personal life this February. There are a lot of domestic tasks on your agenda – fixing up your home, repairs, buying or selling real estate. In some cases, you might receive an inheritance.

Families are feeling stable this month. Some slight friction is likely at the beginning and end of the month, possibly related to how busy you are with your house.

Even divorced couples might find themselves getting along well enough to deal with some material issues.

Health. This month, you are feeling energetic and have no reason to fear falling ill, especially if you do not overeat and take time to walk around in nature. This is especially relevant if you tend toward weight gain.

March

New York Time			London Time		
Calendar Day	Lunar Day	Lunar Day Start Time	Calendar Day	Lunar Day	Lunar Day Start Time
01/03/2022	29	5:53 AM	01/03/2022	29	6:15 AM
02/03/2022	30	6:25 AM	02/03/2022	30	6:39 AM
02/03/2022	1	12:38 PM	02/03/2022	1	5:38 PM
03/03/2022	2	6:54 AM	03/03/2022	2	7:00 AM
04/03/2022	3	7:22 AM	04/03/2022	3	7:19 AM
05/03/2022	4	7:49 AM	05/03/2022	4	7:38 AM
06/03/2022	5	8:18 AM	06/03/2022	5	7:57 AM
07/03/2022	6	8:48 AM	07/03/2022	6	8:19 AM
08/03/2022	7	9:22 AM	08/03/2022	7	8:45 AM
09/03/2022	8	10:00 AM	09/03/2022	8	9:16 AM
10/03/2022	9	10:43 AM	10/03/2022	9	9:54 AM
11/03/2022	10	11:31 AM	11/03/2022	10	10:40 AM
12/03/2022	11	12:25 PM	12/03/2022	11	11:34 AM
13/03/2022	12	1:23 PM	13/03/2022	12	12:36 PM
14/03/2022	13	2:24 PM	14/03/2022	13	1:44 PM
15/03/2022	14	3:27 PM	15/03/2022	14	2:55 PM
16/03/2022	15	4:32 PM	16/03/2022	15	4:08 PM
17/03/2022	16	5:38 PM	17/03/2022	16	5:23 PM
18/03/2022	17	6:45 PM	18/03/2022	17	6:39 PM
19/03/2022	18	7:54 PM	19/03/2022	18	7:57 PM
20/03/2022	19	9:05 PM	20/03/2022	19	9:17 PM
21/03/2022	20	10:16 PM	21/03/2022	20	10:37 PM
22/03/2022	21	11:26 PM	22/03/2022	21	11:57 PM
24/03/2022	22	12:34 AM	24/03/2022	22	1:10 AM
25/03/2022	23	1:35 AM	25/03/2022	23	2:14 AM
26/03/2022	24	2:28 AM	26/03/2022	24	3:06 AM
27/03/2022	25	3:13 AM	27/03/2022	25	4:46 AM
28/03/2022	26	3:52 AM	28/03/2022	26	5:17 AM
29/03/2022	27	4:25 AM	29/03/2022	27	5:42 AM
30/03/2022	28	4:54 AM	30/03/2022	28	6:04 AM
31/03/2022	29	5:22 AM	31/03/2022	29	6:23 AM

You can find the description of each lunar day in the chapter "A Guide to The Moon Cycle and Lunar Days"

You are looking at an active, exciting month ahead. Your motto in March is "less talking, more doing!" If you keep that in mind, you can move mountains!

Work. Despite a series of challenges, which are very likely in the beginning of the month, you are making notable progress at work.

Employees are able to strengthen their position at work, which will certainly be reflected in their finances, which will see significant improvements.

Entrepreneurs who are striving for development and expanding their business are able to resolve a series of thorny matters related to real estate, either in whole or in part.

If you experience any ups and downs along the way, you will be able to resolve them if you harness any opportunity, both financial and legal. You still have people with power and influence on your side, as well as old friends.

Money. Your financial situation looks very stable in March. Money will be coming in regularly, and the amount will significantly increase. In addition to your usual income, you can also count on additional sources this month. For example, someone will pay you back a loan, or you might receive a bonus or payment for some extra work.

You are likely to receive some credit or additional profits from various real estate transactions. Expect to receive the largest amounts on March 2, 3, 6-8, 21, 22, 27, and 28.

Love and family. Your personal life has become extremely complicated. You have a very high risk of conflict this month, and the greatest source of tension is none other than you. You are inherently abrupt, emotional, and unpredictable in March, and that might provoke a strong reaction from your loved ones. In the most difficult cases, you might see a truly revolutionary scene play out when things finally come to a head.

A variety of arguments related to real estate are also on the horizon, and they are a continuation of problems that began in the past. Some issues will be resolved this month, but the stars believe not everything will be fixed, and you will be grappling with this again later on.

Just remember that your risk diminishes with each step you take, and eventually, you will be able to reach a favorable end to this journey. Remember that you can't win if you don't try, and don't let yourself forget that!

Spouses suffering from trust issues and anyone else who feels like they are sitting on the fence need to make a choice, given that being able to hold onto old ties as well as new love is highly unlikely.

Health. This month, you are feeling energetic, though the stars recommend that you use this only for peaceful purposes. Your mood swings and emotional outbursts this month will have a negative effect on all areas of your life.

April

New York Time				London Time		
Calendar Day	Lunar Day	Lunar Day Start Time		Calendar Day	Lunar Day	Lunar Day Start Time
01/04/2022	1	1:27 AM		01/04/2022	30	6:41 AM
01/04/2022	2	5:49 AM		01/04/2022	1	7:27 AM
02/04/2022	3	6:17 AM		02/04/2022	2	7:00 AM
03/04/2022	4	6:47 AM		03/04/2022	3	7:21 AM
04/04/2022	5	7:19 AM		04/04/2022	4	7:45 AM
05/04/2022	6	7:55 AM		05/04/2022	5	8:14 AM
06/04/2022	7	8:37 AM		06/04/2022	6	8:49 AM
07/04/2022	8	9:23 AM		07/04/2022	7	9:32 AM
08/04/2022	9	10:14 AM		08/04/2022	8	10:23 AM
09/04/2022	10	11:10 AM		09/04/2022	9	11:22 AM
10/04/2022	11	12:09 PM		10/04/2022	10	12:26 PM
11/04/2022	12	1:11 PM		11/04/2022	11	1:35 PM
12/04/2022	13	2:14 PM		12/04/2022	12	2:46 PM
13/04/2022	14	3:19 PM		13/04/2022	13	4:00 PM
14/04/2022	15	4:26 PM		14/04/2022	14	5:15 PM
15/04/2022	16	5:35 PM		15/04/2022	15	6:33 PM
16/04/2022	17	6:46 PM		16/04/2022	16	7:54 PM
17/04/2022	18	7:59 PM		17/04/2022	17	9:16 PM
18/04/2022	19	9:12 PM		18/04/2022	18	10:39 PM
19/04/2022	20	10:23 PM		19/04/2022	19	11:58 PM
20/04/2022	21	11:29 PM		21/04/2022	20	1:07 AM
22/04/2022	22	12:25 AM		22/04/2022	21	2:04 AM
23/04/2022	23	1:13 AM		23/04/2022	22	2:48 AM
24/04/2022	24	1:53 AM		24/04/2022	23	3:21 AM
25/04/2022	25	2:28 AM		25/04/2022	24	3:48 AM
26/04/2022	26	2:58 AM		26/04/2022	25	4:10 AM
27/04/2022	27	3:25 AM		27/04/2022	26	4:29 AM
28/04/2022	28	3:52 AM		28/04/2022	27	4:47 AM
29/04/2022	29	4:19 AM		29/04/2022	28	5:05 AM
30/04/2022	30	4:47 AM		30/04/2022	29	5:25 AM
30/04/2022	1	4:30 PM		30/04/2022	1	9:30 PM

You can find the description of each lunar day in the chapter "A Guide to The Moon Cycle and Lunar Days"

All month long, you are active, curious, and enterprising. That is reflected in every area of your life, whether at home or at work.

Work. Overall, April is a promising time for establishing contacts with your management, as well as resolving any legal problems that may have cropped up in the recent past.

For the umpteenth time, you will have to discuss difficult issues related to real estate, land, or any other large property, but you will resolve them favorably. In some cases, you may receive financial compensation, while in others, you may sell based on mutual agreement. You are entering what look like very reasonable arrangements, so compromise is both desirable and likely.

Your ties to colleagues from other cities or abroad are moving along nicely, and you might go on a successful trip. Entrepreneurs can expect to reach a beneficial agreement with pleasing financial results.

Money. When it comes to your financial relationships, April is one of the best months of the year. In addition to your usual income, you might see additional profits from various real estate transactions. That may be related to professional activities, or perhaps events in your personal life.

You can expect to receive the largest sums on April 8, 9, 17, 18, and 22-27.

Love and family. Your personal life is predictable and fairly calm. This month, you will need to tackle a lot of household tasks, which have been scheduled since the beginning of winter, if not earlier. These are jobs related to furnishings in your home, summer home, or apartment. You might find yourself increasingly immersed in these tasks closer to the end of April, and continuing into May.

Your relationships with relatives will become very important, and you may meet with family members who live in another city or abroad.

Mars and Venus will be in your sign during the first ten days of the month, along with Saturn. That all means that you are likely to rekindle things with an old flame, reconnect with an old friend, or even meet up with a lover in another city or abroad.

Fate will give you several opportunities to find love, so take advantage of them, if you don't have anyone special in your life right now.

Health. This month, you are feeling a lot more energetic, though Saturn's passing through your sign means that you should maintain a healthy lifestyle and try not to overdo either food or drink.

Those suffering from chronic heart disease should be very careful this month.

May

New York Time			London Time		
Calendar Day	Lunar Day	Lunar Day Start Time	Calendar Day	Lunar Day	Lunar Day Start Time
01/05/2022	2	6:18 AM	01/05/2022	2	5:48 AM
02/05/2022	3	6:53 AM	02/05/2022	3	6:14 AM
03/05/2022	4	7:32 AM	03/05/2022	4	6:47 AM
04/05/2022	5	8:16 AM	04/05/2022	5	7:27 AM
05/05/2022	6	9:06 AM	05/05/2022	6	8:14 AM
06/05/2022	7	10:00 AM	06/05/2022	7	9:10 AM
07/05/2022	8	10:57 AM	07/05/2022	8	10:12 AM
08/05/2022	9	11:57 AM	08/05/2022	9	11:18 AM
09/05/2022	10	12:59 PM	09/05/2022	10	12:27 PM
10/05/2022	11	2:02 PM	10/05/2022	11	1:38 PM
11/05/2022	12	3:06 PM	11/05/2022	12	2:51 PM
12/05/2022	13	4:13 PM	12/05/2022	13	4:07 PM
13/05/2022	14	5:22 PM	13/05/2022	14	5:25 PM
14/05/2022	15	6:34 PM	14/05/2022	15	6:47 PM
15/05/2022	16	7:49 PM	15/05/2022	16	8:11 PM
16/05/2022	17	9:03 PM	16/05/2022	17	9:34 PM
17/05/2022	18	10:14 PM	17/05/2022	18	10:50 PM
18/05/2022	19	11:16 PM	18/05/2022	19	11:55 PM
20/05/2022	20	12:10 AM	20/05/2022	20	12:46 AM
21/05/2022	21	12:53 AM	21/05/2022	21	1:24 AM
22/05/2022	22	1:30 AM	22/05/2022	22	1:53 AM
23/05/2022	23	2:01 AM	23/05/2022	23	2:16 AM
24/05/2022	24	2:30 AM	24/05/2022	24	2:36 AM
25/05/2022	25	2:56 AM	25/05/2022	25	2:54 AM
26/05/2022	26	3:23 AM	26/05/2022	26	3:12 AM
27/05/2022	27	3:50 AM	27/05/2022	27	3:31 AM
28/05/2022	28	4:20 AM	28/05/2022	28	3:52 AM
29/05/2022	29	4:53 AM	29/05/2022	29	4:17 AM
30/05/2022	30	5:30 AM	30/05/2022	30	4:47 AM
30/05/2022	1	7:32 AM	30/05/2022	1	12:32 PM
31/05/2022	2	6:13 AM	31/05/2022	2	5:24 AM

You can find the description of each lunar day in the chapter "A Guide to The Moon Cycle and Lunar Days"

May is a time for you to sit back and take a look around. You can forget about work for a moment, and focus on your home and family. After all, we don't live to work, we work to live!

Work. The most stubborn workaholics who are convinced that everything will come to a standstill without them, might be busy with various everyday administrative tasks in May. You might be finalizing some real estate issues that have been troubling you or resolving some difficult financial matters. This is the case for managers and entrepreneurs at every level.

Even if they remain at work, employees will find their minds constantly wandering to their personal life and family, so the stars recommend taking a few days off and doing what you really want to be doing, right now.

From May 10 to June 3, Mercury will be in retrograde, which means this is a bad time to be signing any important documents, starting a new business, or even meeting new people. Any major deals might be held up for various reasons, for example, the people you need will suddenly be unavailable.

Money. Your bank account is looking healthy, this month. You will be getting income regularly, and not only from your employment. Many Aquarians will receive a handsome profit from real estate transactions, support from your parents, or loved ones.

An inheritance is looking very likely.

Expect to receive the largest amounts on May 1, 5, 6, 15, 16, 23, 24, and 27-29.

Love and family. Many Aquarians are going to be immersed in their home and family life, this month. You might see some real estate transactions – some will be getting a home, apartment, or summer home in order, others will be selling or acquiring a new residence.

Many will also make plans related to a move to another city or even abroad, but for now, things are in the planning stages, and will become a reality sometime during 2022 or 2023.

The best time for meeting new romantic partners is the first ten days of the month. During this time, single people might meet someone special while traveling or among friends who have come from faraway. From May 10 to June 3, you might run into old friends, former flames, and just people you haven't seen in a long time.

Your relationship with relatives will get much better, and you might even meet up with those who have been living in another city or abroad.

Health. This month, you are feeling fairly energetic and have no reason to fear falling ill. You might start gaining weight, so watch your diet and make sure to exercise regularly. Take some long walks in nature.

June

New York Time			London Time		
Calendar Day	Lunar Day	Lunar Day Start Time	Calendar Day	Lunar Day	Lunar Day Start Time
01/06/2022	3	7:00 AM	01/06/2022	3	6:09 AM
02/06/2022	4	7:53 AM	02/06/2022	4	7:02 AM
03/06/2022	5	8:49 AM	03/06/2022	5	8:02 AM
04/06/2022	6	9:48 AM	04/06/2022	6	9:06 AM
05/06/2022	7	10:48 AM	05/06/2022	7	10:14 AM
06/06/2022	8	11:49 AM	06/06/2022	8	11:23 AM
07/06/2022	9	12:51 PM	07/06/2022	9	12:33 PM
08/06/2022	10	1:55 PM	08/06/2022	10	1:45 PM
09/06/2022	11	3:01 PM	09/06/2022	11	3:00 PM
10/06/2022	12	4:10 PM	10/06/2022	12	4:18 PM
11/06/2022	13	5:22 PM	11/06/2022	13	5:39 PM
12/06/2022	14	6:37 PM	12/06/2022	14	7:03 PM
13/06/2022	15	7:50 PM	13/06/2022	15	8:24 PM
14/06/2022	16	8:58 PM	14/06/2022	16	9:36 PM
15/06/2022	17	9:58 PM	15/06/2022	17	10:35 PM
16/06/2022	18	10:47 PM	16/06/2022	18	11:20 PM
17/06/2022	19	11:28 PM	17/06/2022	19	11:54 PM
19/06/2022	20	12:03 AM	19/06/2022	20	12:20 AM
20/06/2022	21	12:33 AM	20/06/2022	21	12:42 AM
21/06/2022	22	1:00 AM	21/06/2022	22	1:01 AM
22/06/2022	23	1:27 AM	22/06/2022	23	1:19 AM
23/06/2022	24	1:54 AM	23/06/2022	24	1:38 AM
24/06/2022	25	2:23 AM	24/06/2022	25	1:58 AM
25/06/2022	26	2:54 AM	25/06/2022	26	2:21 AM
26/06/2022	27	3:30 AM	26/06/2022	27	2:49 AM
27/06/2022	28	4:11 AM	27/06/2022	28	3:24 AM
28/06/2022	29	4:57 AM	28/06/2022	29	4:06 AM
28/06/2022	1	10:53 PM	29/06/2022	1	3:53 AM
29/06/2022	2	5:48 AM	29/06/2022	2	4:56 AM
30/06/2022	3	6:43 AM	30/06/2022	3	5:54 AM

You can find the description of each lunar day in the chapter "A Guide to The Moon Cycle and Lunar Days"

In June, the door to the future is opening, but very soon, you will see what is behind it. You have a real chance at changing your life, and nothing is stopping you from grabbing the brass ring.

Work. The challenges that you dealt with in the past are finally resolved. Entrepreneurs and managers resolve thorny issues involving real estate, land, or other major property.

Employees will be able to carry out their longstanding plans, especially if they are related to travel to different places and countries. Your ties with colleagues from faraway are developing, and this is the main trend this month.

You will reconnect with former partners, and are likely to meet some new colleagues, as well. You can expect a successful trip, as well as plans related to a move, such as working in another city or abroad.

Money. Your finances are stable right now. In addition to your usual income, many Aquarians will also receive additional profits from various real estate transactions. You might also get help from parents, a spouse, or an elderly family member.

Love and family. When it comes to personal matters, you can expect to run into people from your ancient past. An old flame might suddenly show up, but the relationship is unlikely to last for long. Right now, you are looking ahead, and aren't very interested in the past.

In addition to former relationships in mid-June you are also likely to meet someone new. Generally speaking, you won't be bored, as single people with a thirst for adventure are assured a tumultuous personal life, this month.

People with a stable family life will be busy with children, as well as day-to-day issues that piled up over the spring.

Your relationship with relatives has been difficult recently, and things are looking up. Many Aquarians will spend the year making up with a hostile relative.

Both married and unmarried couples might go on a trip in June, and it will be a great success. Some Aquarians will make plans related to moving in 2023, and things will be looking favorable.

This is a good month for studying, especially if you plan to do it in another city or abroad.

Health. This month, your energy levels are high, and you have no reason to fear any diseases. On the contrary, you are feeling so cheerful you will energize anyone you come across.

July

New York Time			London Time		
Calendar Day	Lunar Day	Lunar Day Start Time	Calendar Day	Lunar Day	Lunar Day Start Time
01/07/2022	4	7:41 AM	01/07/2022	4	6:57 AM
02/07/2022	5	8:41 AM	02/07/2022	5	8:04 AM
03/07/2022	6	9:41 AM	03/07/2022	6	9:12 AM
04/07/2022	7	10:42 AM	04/07/2022	7	10:22 AM
05/07/2022	8	11:44 AM	05/07/2022	8	11:32 AM
06/07/2022	9	12:47 PM	06/07/2022	9	12:44 PM
07/07/2022	10	1:53 PM	07/07/2022	10	1:58 PM
08/07/2022	11	3:01 PM	08/07/2022	11	3:15 PM
09/07/2022	12	4:13 PM	09/07/2022	12	4:35 PM
10/07/2022	13	5:25 PM	10/07/2022	13	5:56 PM
11/07/2022	14	6:35 PM	11/07/2022	14	7:12 PM
12/07/2022	15	7:40 PM	12/07/2022	15	8:18 PM
13/07/2022	16	8:35 PM	13/07/2022	16	9:10 PM
14/07/2022	17	9:21 PM	14/07/2022	17	9:50 PM
15/07/2022	18	9:59 PM	15/07/2022	18	10:20 PM
16/07/2022	19	10:32 PM	16/07/2022	19	10:45 PM
17/07/2022	20	11:02 PM	17/07/2022	20	11:05 PM
18/07/2022	21	11:29 PM	18/07/2022	21	11:25 PM
19/07/2022	22	11:57 PM	19/07/2022	22	11:43 PM
21/07/2022	23	12:25 AM	21/07/2022	23	12:03 AM
22/07/2022	24	12:56 AM	22/07/2022	24	12:26 AM
23/07/2022	25	1:31 AM	23/07/2022	25	12:52 AM
24/07/2022	26	2:10 AM	24/07/2022	26	1:25 AM
25/07/2022	27	2:54 AM	25/07/2022	27	2:04 AM
26/07/2022	28	3:43 AM	26/07/2022	28	2:52 AM
27/07/2022	29	4:37 AM	27/07/2022	29	3:47 AM
28/07/2022	30	5:35 AM	28/07/2022	30	4:49 AM
28/07/2022	1	1:55 PM	28/07/2022	1	6:55 PM
29/07/2022	2	6:34 AM	29/07/2022	2	5:55 AM
30/07/2022	3	7:35 AM	30/07/2022	3	7:04 AM
31/07/2022	4	8:36 AM	31/07/2022	4	8:13 AM

You can find the description of each lunar day in the chapter "A Guide to The Moon Cycle and Lunar Days"

A crane in the sky is always more attractive than a sparrow in your hand. Though in order to reach the crane, you're going to have to build a high ladder and check each rung. In other words – roll up your sleeves and get to work!

Work. The doors to a better future have been opened. Those who want to expand their business to another city or abroad will be working with colleagues from afar, and this month things will be moving along, slowly but surely overcoming various obstacles, which are not as fundamental as they may seem at first glance. You may have to finish up some current issues and clarify some things. The situation will improve the last ten days of the month, and by August, you will see that you are on the right track.

Closer to the end of the month or in August you may take a trip, which will be very successful.

Those busy with thorny issues related to real estate will continue to resolve these longstanding problems. Things will gradually stabilize and finally come to an end.

Money. In July, your finances are looking very stable, and money will be coming in regularly, in slightly higher amounts. Entrepreneurs and managers may receive money from various real estate transactions, and those who are not part of the business world will resolve some issues related to that, and also receive a decent sum. Expect the largest amounts on July 8, 9, 16-18, 26, and 27.

Love and family. In your personal life, you will continue to deal with things that began in the recent past. Many Aquarians will be fully immersed with details from their day to day life. That might involve major home improvements, or acquiring or selling an apartment, home, or cottage. Household matters will take precedence, but that doesn't mean there won't be any romance!

Those who already have a long-term partner might work together on boring, household issues, and those who are still single might start talking to a very pleasant person.

Closer to the end of the month or in August, you might meet someone on a trip or among people who have come from faraway.

Your children will make you happy and your relationship with them will be unusually peaceful and harmonious.

Health. July is a great time to finally focus on your body and understand what you actually need. Maybe you will decide to get some testing done and begin eating a healthy diet. Luckily, it's summer and you will have plenty of opportunities.

Elderly people and those who have been weakened by disease should try to prevent any chronic issues. If you can, spend some time at a health resort.

August

New York Time				London Time		
Calendar Day	Lunar Day	Lunar Day Start Time		Calendar Day	Lunar Day	Lunar Day Start Time
01/08/2022	5	9:37 AM		01/08/2022	5	9:23 AM
02/08/2022	6	10:40 AM		02/08/2022	6	10:34 AM
03/08/2022	7	11:44 AM		03/08/2022	7	11:46 AM
04/08/2022	8	12:49 PM		04/08/2022	8	1:00 PM
05/08/2022	9	1:58 PM		05/08/2022	9	2:17 PM
06/08/2022	10	3:07 PM		06/08/2022	10	3:35 PM
07/08/2022	11	4:16 PM		07/08/2022	11	4:51 PM
08/08/2022	12	5:22 PM		08/08/2022	12	6:00 PM
09/08/2022	13	6:20 PM		09/08/2022	13	6:58 PM
10/08/2022	14	7:10 PM		10/08/2022	14	7:43 PM
11/08/2022	15	7:52 PM		11/08/2022	15	8:17 PM
12/08/2022	16	8:28 PM		12/08/2022	16	8:45 PM
13/08/2022	17	9:00 PM		13/08/2022	17	9:07 PM
14/08/2022	18	9:29 PM		14/08/2022	18	9:28 PM
15/08/2022	19	9:57 PM		15/08/2022	19	9:47 PM
16/08/2022	20	10:26 PM		16/08/2022	20	10:07 PM
17/08/2022	21	10:56 PM		17/08/2022	21	10:29 PM
18/08/2022	22	11:30 PM		18/08/2022	22	10:54 PM
20/08/2022	23	12:08 AM		19/08/2022	23	11:25 PM
21/08/2022	24	12:50 AM		21/08/2022	24	12:02 AM
22/08/2022	25	1:38 AM		22/08/2022	25	12:46 AM
23/08/2022	26	2:30 AM		23/08/2022	26	1:39 AM
24/08/2022	27	3:27 AM		24/08/2022	27	2:39 AM
25/08/2022	28	4:26 AM		25/08/2022	28	3:45 AM
26/08/2022	29	5:27 AM		26/08/2022	29	4:53 AM
27/08/2022	1	4:16 AM		26/08/2022	30	6:02 AM
27/08/2022	2	6:28 AM		27/08/2022	1	9:16 AM
28/08/2022	3	7:30 AM		28/08/2022	2	7:13 AM
29/08/2022	4	8:33 AM		29/08/2022	3	8:24 AM
30/08/2022	5	9:37 AM		30/08/2022	4	9:36 AM
31/08/2022	6	10:42 AM		31/08/2022	5	10:50 AM

You can find the description of each lunar day in the chapter "A Guide to The Moon Cycle and Lunar Days"

In August, you will once again be dealing with issues that you had resolved long ago. You are handling it your own way – intelligently, creatively, and enthusiastically.

Work. Your main achievement this month will be expanding your circle of acquaintances. Most likely, that will take place while traveling or with people who have come from faraway. This is a very promising relationship during the first week of August.

In mid-August, from the 7th to 14th, you may face a series of problems that you have seen before. This time, however, they may be unexpectedly acute. This likely involves real estate, land, or other property. Even if you believe the situation is absolutely resolved, nothing will stop your opponents from bringing them up again.

There may be a silver lining, however, in that it will allow you to understand where you and your opponents stand. The new moon will be in Virgo on August 27, which will allow you to strengthen your position and once again fend off your opponents.

Money. Your financial situation is looking rather neutral in August. You do not have any major windfalls on the horizon, but your expenses will be modest, as always.

Love and family. If your personal life is much more important to you than work, here you can expect both advantages and drawbacks. The advantages include a better relationship with your relatives; possible travel, and reconnecting with family members who live in other cities or abroad.

The drawbacks might include constant difficulties related to real estate, which come up over and over again. Nothing is new here, though, and you are able to ward off any enemies' machinations. This concerns both stable marriages and divorcing couples.

Couples who are dating will face issues with one of their parents or an elderly family member. In order to avoid being completely bogged down with household and everyday squabbles, maybe take a trip. There will be an opportunity in August. This will allow you to relax and get a better look at things.

Health. Right now, you are in good shape and have no reason to fear falling ill. The exception to that is those who suffer from chronic diseases, who should go get a good massage and do some light stretching in the morning.

September

New York Time			London Time		
Calendar Day	Lunar Day	Lunar Day Start Time	Calendar Day	Lunar Day	Lunar Day Start Time
01/09/2022	7	11:49 AM	01/09/2022	6	12:06 PM
02/09/2022	8	12:57 PM	02/09/2022	7	1:23 PM
03/09/2022	9	2:05 PM	03/09/2022	8	2:38 PM
04/09/2022	10	3:10 PM	04/09/2022	9	3:48 PM
05/09/2022	11	4:10 PM	05/09/2022	10	4:48 PM
06/09/2022	12	5:01 PM	06/09/2022	11	5:37 PM
07/09/2022	13	5:45 PM	07/09/2022	12	6:14 PM
08/09/2022	14	6:23 PM	08/09/2022	13	6:44 PM
09/09/2022	15	6:56 PM	09/09/2022	14	7:08 PM
10/09/2022	16	7:26 PM	10/09/2022	15	7:30 PM
11/09/2022	17	7:55 PM	11/09/2022	16	7:50 PM
12/09/2022	18	8:24 PM	12/09/2022	17	8:10 PM
13/09/2022	19	8:54 PM	13/09/2022	18	8:31 PM
14/09/2022	20	9:27 PM	14/09/2022	19	8:55 PM
15/09/2022	21	10:04 PM	15/09/2022	20	9:24 PM
16/09/2022	22	10:45 PM	16/09/2022	21	9:58 PM
17/09/2022	23	11:31 PM	17/09/2022	22	10:40 PM
19/09/2022	24	12:22 AM	18/09/2022	23	11:30 PM
20/09/2022	25	1:17 AM	20/09/2022	24	12:28 AM
21/09/2022	26	2:15 AM	21/09/2022	25	1:31 AM
22/09/2022	27	3:15 AM	22/09/2022	26	2:38 AM
23/09/2022	28	4:17 AM	23/09/2022	27	3:47 AM
24/09/2022	29	5:19 AM	24/09/2022	28	4:58 AM
25/09/2022	30	6:22 AM	25/09/2022	29	6:10 AM
25/09/2022	1	5:54 PM	25/09/2022	1	10:54 PM
26/09/2022	2	7:27 AM	26/09/2022	2	7:23 AM
27/09/2022	3	8:33 AM	27/09/2022	3	8:38 AM
28/09/2022	4	9:40 AM	28/09/2022	4	9:54 AM
29/09/2022	5	10:49 AM	29/09/2022	5	11:12 AM
30/09/2022	6	11:58 AM	30/09/2022	6	12:29 PM

You can find the description of each lunar day in the chapter "A Guide to The Moon Cycle and Lunar Days"

This month, you will understand that the path to the top is becoming more difficult and even the slightest movement forward requires incredible effort on your part. But that doesn't mean you should give up on your goals and do nothing! Take a break, take a step back and look around, and then get ready to continue charging ahead!

Work. The first 10 days of September are the best time of the month. During this time, you might take a trip, and be active when negotiating with colleagues in other cities or abroad. However, during the last 20 days of the month, you may notice that many projects that had been developing successfully in August and early September, have suddenly come to a halt. A series of obstacles now lie in your path, and this may look differently, depending on your field and your future plans.

Those planning on a move or collaborating with colleagues in other cities or abroad will run into difficulties. They may involve the laws of another country, or perhaps strange, erratic behavior from a colleague from faraway. Alternatively, you may see old legal troubles rear their heads again, or unexpected new ones may appear. In either case, remember that this month, and in the future, it is not worth breaking any laws. Be careful and follow any instructions you are given in order to avoid any problems that might haunt you until winter.

Money. Your financial situation is looking rather neutral this month. You will not receive any windfalls, but you will be able to avoid a lot of expenses. The astrologist predicts that most of the expenses you do have will be related to your personal life and family-related problems.

Love and family. Your personal life is looking uneven and turbulent in September. Families may face problems involving their children, and this may not come cheap. As you jump forward, you can say that any problems that come up this month may drag on, so it is worth giving your children's issues the attention they deserve.

Some difficult issues related to real estate may now be in their final stages of being resolved. Even if they appeared to have already been put away, there may still be some loose ends to tie up, and it may take more work than you anticipated.

In many families, there may be some tension involving relatives. You might find yourself in a huge argument with several of your loved ones. Alternatively, a relative might fall ill or suffer a very difficult period, and if that is the case, they will need some help, whether moral or financial.

September is a very difficult time for unmarried couples. A recent romance will suddenly cool down and you will fall back down to earth with a thud. The cause will be hard to predict, but there will probably be a reason for your dissatisfaction in one another. If the relationship means anything to you, then watch your tongue and control yourself as much as you can.

Health. In September, you are feeling less than energetic, so take care of yourself and remember that moderation is key. Be very careful when traveling and driving, as the last 20 days of the month will be the most dangerous time.

October

New York Time				London Time		
Calendar Day	Lunar Day	Lunar Day Start Time		Calendar Day	Lunar Day	Lunar Day Start Time
01/10/2022	7	1:04 PM		01/10/2022	7	1:41 PM
02/10/2022	8	2:04 PM		02/10/2022	8	2:44 PM
03/10/2022	9	2:57 PM		03/10/2022	9	3:35 PM
04/10/2022	10	3:43 PM		04/10/2022	10	4:15 PM
05/10/2022	11	4:21 PM		05/10/2022	11	4:46 PM
06/10/2022	12	4:55 PM		06/10/2022	12	5:11 PM
07/10/2022	13	5:25 PM		07/10/2022	13	5:33 PM
08/10/2022	14	5:54 PM		08/10/2022	14	5:53 PM
09/10/2022	15	6:23 PM		09/10/2022	15	6:12 PM
10/10/2022	16	6:52 PM		10/10/2022	16	6:33 PM
11/10/2022	17	7:24 PM		11/10/2022	17	6:55 PM
12/10/2022	18	7:59 PM		12/10/2022	18	7:22 PM
13/10/2022	19	8:39 PM		13/10/2022	19	7:54 PM
14/10/2022	20	9:23 PM		14/10/2022	20	8:34 PM
15/10/2022	21	10:12 PM		15/10/2022	21	9:21 PM
16/10/2022	22	11:06 PM		16/10/2022	22	10:16 PM
18/10/2022	23	12:03 AM		17/10/2022	23	11:17 PM
19/10/2022	24	1:02 AM		19/10/2022	24	12:22 AM
20/10/2022	25	2:03 AM		20/10/2022	25	1:30 AM
21/10/2022	26	3:04 AM		21/10/2022	26	2:39 AM
22/10/2022	27	4:06 AM		22/10/2022	27	3:50 AM
23/10/2022	28	5:10 AM		23/10/2022	28	5:03 AM
24/10/2022	29	6:16 AM		24/10/2022	29	6:18 AM
25/10/2022	1	6:48 AM		25/10/2022	30	7:35 AM
25/10/2022	2	7:25 AM		25/10/2022	1	11:48 AM
26/10/2022	3	8:35 AM		26/10/2022	2	8:54 AM
27/10/2022	4	9:46 AM		27/10/2022	3	10:14 AM
28/10/2022	5	10:55 AM		28/10/2022	4	11:30 AM
29/10/2022	6	11:59 AM		29/10/2022	5	12:38 PM
30/10/2022	7	12:55 PM		30/10/2022	6	12:33 PM
31/10/2022	8	1:42 PM		31/10/2022	7	1:16 PM

You can find the description of each lunar day in the chapter "A Guide to The Moon Cycle and Lunar Days"

In October, you are slowly but surely scaling the mountain. In addition to progressing at work, you might also make a real leap, spiritually and when it comes to understanding yourself, the world, and others.

Work. This is a very successful month for you at work. You might be actively working with colleagues from other cities and abroad, or even go on a trip.

Difficult issues that have been bothering you recently will look much more manageable and like something you can resolve. This goes for problems involving your colleagues from afar as well as any legal issues.

Those with problems involving land or other real estate disputes might once again face a new round of demands from opponents, but you will be able to skillfully overcome this. This is a story that has been going on for some time now, and each time, you are able to find the right argument and support it with irrefutable facts. This will be the case this time, and everything will be resolved favorably closer to the end of the month, when things are clearer.

October is a great time for studying, learning new things, and a job. In some cases, this will take place in another city or abroad.

Money. Your finances are looking rather neutral this month. You will not have a lot of income, but your expenses will be reasonable, predictable, and mostly related to your family, children, and loved ones.

Things will be looking up in late October, when Jupiter, the planet of success, will return to the financial sector of your sky. If you do not receive money in late October, wait until November, when it is sure to show up.

Love and family. Things are also improving in your personal life. After some recent disagreements, couples will be able to find a path to each other's hearts. You might take a trip, which will bring you closer together if your relationship suffered in September.

Parents will strengthen their relationship with children, and visit them if they are currently studying or living in another city or abroad. Your children still need your support, both financially and morally. This situation is unlikely to change anytime soon, and it's true that children are like flowers, water them daily with love and watch them bloom.

Those dealing with challenges related to real estate will be able to grapple with these issues in mid-October. The situation is not hopeless – resolving it is taking some time, but with each step, you are closer to getting your way. Keep a cool head, act methodically, and you will see success.

Health. In October, you are noticeably more energetic, and you are also improving your confidence and mood. Even if you were recently ill, you will make a quick recovery.

November

New York Time			London Time		
Calendar Day	Lunar Day	Lunar Day Start Time	Calendar Day	Lunar Day	Lunar Day Start Time
01/11/2022	9	2:23 PM	01/11/2022	8	1:50 PM
02/11/2022	10	2:57 PM	02/11/2022	9	2:16 PM
03/11/2022	11	3:27 PM	03/11/2022	10	2:38 PM
04/11/2022	12	3:56 PM	04/11/2022	11	2:58 PM
05/11/2022	13	4:24 PM	05/11/2022	12	3:17 PM
06/11/2022	14	3:52 PM	06/11/2022	13	3:36 PM
07/11/2022	15	4:22 PM	07/11/2022	14	3:58 PM
08/11/2022	16	4:56 PM	08/11/2022	15	4:22 PM
09/11/2022	17	5:33 PM	09/11/2022	16	4:52 PM
10/11/2022	18	6:16 PM	10/11/2022	17	5:28 PM
11/11/2022	19	7:04 PM	11/11/2022	18	6:12 PM
12/11/2022	20	7:56 PM	12/11/2022	19	7:05 PM
13/11/2022	21	8:52 PM	13/11/2022	20	8:03 PM
14/11/2022	22	9:50 PM	14/11/2022	21	9:07 PM
15/11/2022	23	10:49 PM	15/11/2022	22	10:13 PM
16/11/2022	24	11:49 PM	16/11/2022	23	11:21 PM
18/11/2022	25	12:50 AM	18/11/2022	24	12:30 AM
19/11/2022	26	1:52 AM	19/11/2022	25	1:41 AM
20/11/2022	27	2:56 AM	20/11/2022	26	2:53 AM
21/11/2022	28	4:03 AM	21/11/2022	27	4:09 AM
22/11/2022	29	5:13 AM	22/11/2022	28	5:27 AM
23/11/2022	30	6:25 AM	23/11/2022	29	6:48 AM
23/11/2022	1	5:57 PM	23/11/2022	1	10:57 PM
24/11/2022	2	7:37 AM	24/11/2022	2	8:08 AM
25/11/2022	3	8:45 AM	25/11/2022	3	9:23 AM
26/11/2022	4	9:47 AM	26/11/2022	4	10:25 AM
27/11/2022	5	10:39 AM	27/11/2022	5	11:15 AM
28/11/2022	6	11:23 AM	28/11/2022	6	11:52 AM
29/11/2022	7	12:00 PM	29/11/2022	7	12:21 PM
30/11/2022	8	12:31 PM	30/11/2022	8	12:45 PM

You can find the description of each lunar day in the chapter "A Guide to The Moon Cycle and Lunar Days"

This month, Luck is knocking at your door. And this time, it is taking on a tangible, material shape. Jump on in! Time is on your side!

Work. Professionally speaking, November is one of the best months of the year for you. Entrepreneurs and managers can count on successfully resolving their problems, new projects, and profits from work previously completed.

Employees will have an incredible opportunity to move up the ladder at work, and if that recently took place already, you will have the chance to strengthen your position.

Thorny issues related to disputes over real estate will become less acute, and you may even find an acceptable, favorable resolution for both parties.

If you work in something related to construction, land, or real estate, keep your finger on the pulse of things – there is a high probability of people responsible for this enterprise stepping away from what had been planned.

Money. November is one of the best months of the year for you. For many Aquarians, it may even be your golden hour for money and other material benefits. Expect the largest sums to come in on November 3, 4, 11-13, 22, 23, and 30.

Of course, you have expenses, that is unavoidable, but most of them will be related to your family, children, and loved ones.

Love and family. Your personal life is looking much less positive than things at work.

Spouses might be arguing a lot, and once again, this is due to varying issues related to your home. Alternatively, you might have disagreements caused by parents or older relatives.

Issues related to your home might plague many Aquarians, but this is nothing new and you are used to it by now. You probably already know what to do, and how to put an end to this matter. The stars believe that things are coming to a favorable end.

Your relationship with a partner looks like bad fall weather – little sun and often filled with freezing drizzle. The stars recommend that you get through it, avoid dragging other people into your relationship, and rely on your intelligence, instead.

Health. In November, you are healthy, energetic, and full of strength. You naturally have no reason to fear any illness.

December

New York Time			London Time		
Calendar Day	Lunar Day	Lunar Day Start Time	Calendar Day	Lunar Day	Lunar Day Start Time
01/12/2022	9	1:00 PM	01/12/2022	9	1:05 PM
02/12/2022	10	1:27 PM	02/12/2022	10	1:24 PM
03/12/2022	11	1:55 PM	03/12/2022	11	1:42 PM
04/12/2022	12	2:24 PM	04/12/2022	12	2:03 PM
05/12/2022	13	2:56 PM	05/12/2022	13	2:25 PM
06/12/2022	14	3:31 PM	06/12/2022	14	2:53 PM
07/12/2022	15	4:11 PM	07/12/2022	15	3:26 PM
08/12/2022	16	4:57 PM	08/12/2022	16	4:07 PM
09/12/2022	17	5:48 PM	09/12/2022	17	4:56 PM
10/12/2022	18	6:42 PM	10/12/2022	18	5:53 PM
11/12/2022	19	7:40 PM	11/12/2022	19	6:55 PM
12/12/2022	20	8:39 PM	12/12/2022	20	8:00 PM
13/12/2022	21	9:38 PM	13/12/2022	21	9:07 PM
14/12/2022	22	10:37 PM	14/12/2022	22	10:15 PM
15/12/2022	23	11:37 PM	15/12/2022	23	11:23 PM
17/12/2022	24	12:39 AM	17/12/2022	24	12:32 AM
18/12/2022	25	1:42 AM	18/12/2022	25	1:44 AM
19/12/2022	26	2:49 AM	19/12/2022	26	2:59 AM
20/12/2022	27	3:58 AM	20/12/2022	27	4:18 AM
21/12/2022	28	5:10 AM	21/12/2022	28	5:38 AM
22/12/2022	29	6:22 AM	22/12/2022	29	6:56 AM
23/12/2022	1	5:17 AM	23/12/2022	30	8:07 AM
23/12/2022	2	7:28 AM	23/12/2022	1	10:17 AM
24/12/2022	3	8:27 AM	24/12/2022	2	9:04 AM
25/12/2022	4	9:17 AM	25/12/2022	3	9:49 AM
26/12/2022	5	9:58 AM	26/12/2022	4	10:22 AM
27/12/2022	6	10:32 AM	27/12/2022	5	10:49 AM
28/12/2022	7	11:03 AM	28/12/2022	6	11:11 AM
29/12/2022	8	11:31 AM	29/12/2022	7	11:30 AM
30/12/2022	9	11:59 AM	30/12/2022	8	11:49 AM
31/12/2022	10	12:28 PM	31/12/2022	9	12:09 PM

You can find the description of each lunar day in the chapter "A Guide to The Moon Cycle and Lunar Days"

Your trump card is your ability to react quickly and think out of the box. In December, you will do just that, as this is going to be a very difficult month.

Work. Expect the first half of December to be marred by conflicts and disagreements. This may be due to various material obligations and the warring parties may have differing positions on such a delicate issue. Perhaps they were once friends or at least like-minded individuals, or alternatively, you are dealing with a hostile government body representative. This may be over land, real estate, or other major assets. If during the first half of the month, you are unable to reach an agreement, during the second half, you will be on track to reach your goals. Very soon, you may finally be rid of this exhausting and now ancient problem.

Money. Given your challenges at work, money trouble is all but inevitable. You will be spending constantly and not only on professional issues, but also on your loved ones' and children's needs. As a result, near the end of the month, your bank account will be in the red.

Love and family. If you are more focused on your family life this month, get ready for some Shakespearean drama.

Things look most difficult for unmarried couples – you might be arguing, and your friends and loved ones may get involved, too. Your integrity is being seriously put to the test – it will be clear what is truly important to you, and what you are able to actually give up. What's more, your deal breakers will also become obvious.

Families may experience trouble involving children – perhaps the younger generation will be feeling rather mutinous, or alternatively, your children may be going through difficult times and you will have to help with a kind word and some money.

Difficult issues related to real estate will be resolved, slowly but surely. You will be making some very positive steps in that direction during the second half of December.

Health. In December, many Aquarians will feel like they have been broken down entirely. Work, dealing with professional and personal problems, anxieties- this means that close to the end of the month, you might feel as though you are teetering on the brink.

Take a few days to get away from home, and the endless hustle and bustle. You need a real break for the holidays, more than anyone, so see if you can take some extra days off.

A Guide to The Moon Cycle and Lunar Days

Since Ancient times, people have noticed that the moon has a strong influence on nature. Our Earth and everything living on it is a single living being, which is why the phases of the moon have such an effect on our health and mental state, and therefore, our lives. Remember Shakespeare and his description of Othello's jealousy in his famous tragedy:

"It is the very error of the moon, She comes more nearer Earth than she was wont And makes men mad."

If our inner rhythm is in harmony with that of the cosmos, we are able to achieve much more. People were aware of this a thousand years ago. The lunar calendar is ancient. We can find it among the ancient Sumerians (4000-3000 BC), the inhabitants of Mesopotamia, Native Americans, Hindus, and ancient Slavs. There is evidence that the Siberian Yakuts had a lunar calendar, as did the Malaysians.

Primitive tribes saw the moon as a source of fertility. Long before Christianity, the waxing moon was seen as favorable for planting new crops and starting a new business, for success and making money, while the waning moon was a sign that business would end.

What are the phases of the moon?

- Phase 1 – new moon
- Phase 2 – waxing crescent moon
- Phase 3 – first quarter moon
- Phase 4 – waxing gibbous moon
- Phase 5 – full moon
- Phase 6 – waning gibbous moon
- Phase 7 – third quarter moon
- Phase 8 – waning crescent moon

To simplify things, we can divide the month into two phases:
Waxing crescent moon - before the full moon
Waning crescent moon - after the full moon

New Moon

We cannot see the new moon, as it is hidden. People might complain about feeling weak, mental imbalance, and fatigue. During this time, we want to avoid taking on too much or overdoing things. Generally, people are not very responsive and react poorly to requests, which is why it is best to look out for yourself, while not keeping your plate too full.

The new moon is a bad time for advertising – it will go unnoticed. It is not worth preparing any presentations, parties, or loud gatherings. People are feeling constrained, not very social, and sluggish.

This is also a less than ideal time for surgery, as your recovery will be slow, and the likelihood of medical error is high.

It is also difficult to get an accurate diagnosis during the new moon – diseases might seem to be hidden, and doctors might not see the real underlying cause of what ails you.

The new moon is also a bad time for dates, and sexual encounters may be dissatisfying and leave you feeling disappointed. Ancient astrologers did not advise planning a wedding night during the new moon.

Waxing Crescent Moon

It is easy to identify a waxing crescent moon. If you draw an imaginary line between the two "horns", you should see the letter P. The waxing moon is then divided into one and two quarters.

During the first quarter moon, we need to focus on planning – setting goals and thinking of how we will set about achieving them. However, it is still a good idea to hold back a bit and not overdo things. Energy levels are still low, though they are growing along with the moon. It is still a good idea to avoid any medical procedures during this time.

The second quarter is a time for bold, decisive action. Things will come easy, and there is a greater chance of a lucky break. This is a good time for weddings, especially if the moon will be in Libra, Cancer, or Taurus. Nevertheless, it is a good idea to put off any advertising activities and public speaking until closer to the full moon, if you can.

Full Moon

During the full moon, the Earth is located between the sun and the moon. During this time, the moon is round and fully illuminated. This takes place during days 14-16 of the lunar cycle.

During the full moon, many people feel more vigorous than usual. They are emotional, sociable, and actively seeking more contact, so this may be a good time for any celebrations.

However, be careful not to drink too much – you can relax to the point that you lose control, and the consequences of that can be very unpleasant. If you are able to stick to moderation, there is no better time for a party!

The full moon is also the best time for advertising, as not only will your campaign be widely seen, people will be apt to remember it.

The full moon is also a favorable time for dates, and during this time, people are at their most open, romantic, and willing to tell each other something important that might take their relationship to the next level of trust and understanding.

Moreover, during the full moon, people feel a surge of energy, which may lead to hyperactivity, restlessness, and insomnia.

It will be harder to keep your emotions in check. You might face conflicts with friends, disasters, and accidents. During the full moon, any surgeries are **not a good idea**, as the risk of complications and bleeding is on the rise. Plastic surgery is also a bad idea, as swelling and bruises might be much worse than in another lunar phase. At the same time, the full moon is a good time to get an accurate diagnosis.

During this time, try to limit your calories and liquid intake (especially if you deal with bloating and excess weight), as your body is absorbing both calories and liquids faster during the full moon, and it can be very difficult to get rid of the weight later on.

Waning Crescent Moon

The full moon is over, and a new phase is beginning – the waning moon. This is a quieter time, when all of the jobs you started earlier are being partly or entirely completed (it all depends on the speed and scale).

Surgery will turn out much better if it is performed during the waning moon. Your recovery will be faster, and the likelihood of complications is much lower. If you have any plans to lose weight, the waning moon is the best time to do that. This is also a good time for quitting bad habits, such as smoking or cursing.

The waning moon can also be divided into the third and fourth quarters.

Third quarter - this is a favorable period, and you are able to resolve a lot of problems without conflict. People are calming down and ready to listen and take in information, while still being active. However, this is not the best time to begin any major projects, especially if you are unsure if you will be able to complete them by the start of the new lunar month.

The third quarter is a good time to get married, especially if the moon is in Cancer, Taurus, or Libra.

Fourth quarter – This is the most passive period of the lunar cycle. You are not as strong as usual. Your energy is lagging. You will be tired until reaching a new beginning. The best thing you can do as the lunar cycle comes to an end is to get things in order, and avoid anything that might get in your way at work or in personal relationships. Examine your successes and failures.

Now, let's discuss the lunar days in greater detail. For centuries, people around the world have described the influence of lunar days, and modern astrologers only add to this work, as they compare old texts to modern life.

The 1st lunar day

The first lunar day is extremely important for the rest of the lunar month. This is a much-needed day to carefully plan your activities and lay the groundwork for the rest of the lunar month. Remember that the first lunar day is not a good day for major activities, but rather for sitting down and planning things.

Avoid conflicts on this day, unless you want them to overshadow the rest of the month. Try to see the positive side of things and imagine that the lunar month will bring you good things both at work and in love. The more vividly you can imagine this, the sooner your desires will come to fruition. Perhaps it would be a good idea to jot down plans that will bring you closer to achieving your dreams. This is the best time for both manifesting and making wishes!

This is also a favorable day when it comes to seeking a new job or starting an academic program.

It is fine to go out on a date on the first lunar day, but limit any sexual contact, as your energy levels are low, and you are likely to end up disappointed.

Getting married on the first lunar day is not recommended.

Avoid getting a haircut – there are many indications that cutting your hair on the first lunar day will have a negative effect on your health and life expectancy.

Under no circumstances should you undergo any major cosmetic procedures, including plastic surgery. Energy levels are low, your skin is dull and almost stagnant. The results will not live up to your expectations, and in the worst-case scenario, you will end up looking worse than before. It is common for cosmetic procedures performed on this day to be disappointing or even useless. Even the best surgeons are less capable.

Your good dreams on the first lunar day foretell happiness and joy. Bad ones usually do not come true.

The 2nd lunar day

This is considered a lucky day, and is symbolized by a cornucopia. It is not an exaggeration to say that the second lunar day is a favorable time for both work and love. It is a time for action, and a great period to work on yourself, look for a new job, start something new, or complete any financial transaction, whether a sale or purchase. This is also a great time for creative and scientific insights, and a good time for any meeting – whether political or romantic.

Any romantic dates or sexual encounters during the second lunar day are unlikely to disappoint. This is also a good day for weddings or taking a trip with someone special.

During the second lunar day, the moon is beginning its waxing phase, which is a good time for anything you might to do nourish and restore your skin. This is a great time for any cosmetic procedures aimed at preservation, though it is best to put off any plastic surgery until the waning moon. If that is not possible, then the second lunar day is acceptable, if not ideal, and you will not run into any complications.

Folklore tells us that this is not a good day for a haircut, as that may lead to arguments with a loved one.

This is the best time for exercise – your body is in good shape, and you are able to handle new exercise regimens. If the moon happens to be in Scorpio, though, be careful.

This is a good day for anything positive, but avoid any conflicts, discussions about the status of your relationship, or litigation.

Dreams of the second lunar day are usually not prophetic.

The 3rd lunar day

On this day, we are usually able to make out a thin sliver of the lunar crescent. It is a longstanding tradition to show money during the new month – it is believed that as the moon grows, so will your savings.

However, astrological systems around the world consider this an unlucky, unfavorable day. It is not a good idea to travel, begin any new business, or give into your bad mood.

You might run into many a lot of problems at work on this day, which will cause you a lot of anxiety. However, it is a good day to take a step back and identify and set about fixing any flaws and shortcomings. Remember that everything tends to look worse on this day than it actually is.

It is not the time to ask management for anything – you are likely to walk away disappointed, and end up unfairly reprimanded rather than receiving a promotion or raise. Instead, focus on areas of work that need to be smoothed over or studied further. It will be clear what problems you are facing, and you will easily be able to find a remedy.

Do not rush to criticize your loved ones – things may not be as they appear. "Measure twice and cut once" is your motto on this day.

This is not a good day to get married, as the couple is likely to have a turbulent, short-lived marriage.

You can schedule a cosmetic procedure for this day, but only if it is relatively minor. Plastic surgery should wait.

Do exercises as usual, without overdoing it or adding any new routines.

Dreams on this day do not mean anything.

The 4ᵗʰ lunar day

These are relatively neutral days, in that they are unlikely to bring anything bad, but they also will not bring you any windfalls. The fourth lunar day is symbolized by a tree of paradise, the tree of knowledge, and the choice between good and evil. Things ultimately depend on us and our final decisions.

This is a great day for anything money-related – signing contracts, agreements, or even taking on credit. There are also a lot of contradictions on this day – on one hand, we are likely to receive money, which is a good thing, but on the other, we will have to give some of it away, which is never particularly fun or pleasant. There is good reason to consider all of your opportunities and possibilities before acting.

It is not a good day to get married, as the wedding will not be as fun as you had hoped. However, the fourth lunar day is, in fact, a good day for sex and conceiving a healthy child.

Be careful on this day if you happen to engage in any physical exercise, as it is not a good idea to overeat or abuse alcohol. Take care of yourself.

Any illnesses which began on this day may be extremely dangerous, if they are not dealt with immediately.

Cosmetic procedures are not contraindicated, as long as they are to preserve your appearance. Plastic surgery can be performed if you truly feel it is necessary.

However, avoid getting a haircut, as it is unlikely to grow back healthily, and will become brittle and dull. However, if the moon is in Leo, you can disregard this advice.

Dreams may turn out to be real.

The 5ᵗʰ lunar day

Traditionally, the fifth lunar day is one of the worst of the lunar month. It is symbolized by a unicorn. Unicorns need to be tamed, but only a virgin is capable of doing so. Many people will feel drained on this day, or frustrated with themselves, those around them, and life in general.

Try to avoid arguments- any conflicts are likely to drag out for a long time, and then you may be overcome with guilt. This advice is relevant for both work and love.

Sexual encounters may be pleasant, but this is not a good day to plan a wedding, as it is likely to lead to a marriage full of unpleasant incidents.

Do not start any new businesses, or ask those around you for favors-you may be misunderstood and rejected.

It is fine to engage in physical exercise, but if you overdo it on this day, you may injure yourself.

Your energy levels are low. Cosmetic procedures may not be effective, and avoid any plastic surgeries.

It is good if you dream something connected with the road, trips or with movement in general. A bad dream might be a sign of a health problem which should be addressed.

The 6th lunar day

The symbol of the sixth lunar day is a cloud and a crane. This is a philosophical combination that suggests that it is not worth rushing things on these days. This is a very positive, lucky day for both work and love. Creative work will be especially successful, as will any attempts at opening a new business in your field.

The sixth lunar day is a good time for resolving any financial matters. There is one limitation, however – do not give anyone a loan, as they may not pay it back. But you can certainly sponsor and support those who are more vulnerable than you.

This day is a good time to go on a trip, whether close to home or far away.

This is also a good day for dates, weddings, and marriage proposals. Remember that energy is more romantic than sexual, so it is better to give the gift of roses and a bottle of champagne than hot, passionate sex.

It is a good idea to get some exercise, but do not overdo things, though you will probably not want to, either.

Cosmetic procedures will be successful, and you can even have plastic surgery performed, so long as the moon is not in Scorpio.

It is still a good idea to avoid getting your hair cut, as you might "cut off" something good in addition to your hair.

It is better to not discuss dreams as they are usually true. Your dreams of this day can remind you of something that needs to be completed as soon as possible.

The 7th lunar day

This is also a favorable lunar day, and it is symbolized by a fighting cock, which is an Avestan deity. Avoid any aggression on this day, and instead work on yourself, spend time at home or in nature. Avoid discussing the status of your relationship with anyone, arguing, or wishing bad things on anyone. Everything will come back to haunt you, remember, silence is golden.

Business negotiations and contracts will be successful. You can find support, sponsors, and people ready to help you in both words and deeds.

Lighten up with your colleagues and subordinates. Pay attention not only to their shortcomings, but also to their skills. This is a good day for reconciliation and creating both political and romantic unions.

The seventh lunar day is good for traveling, no matter how near or far from home.

It is also a favorable time for love and marriage.

Exercise moderately, and any plastic surgeries will go very smoothly, as long as the moon is not in Scorpio.

Dreams of this day may become a reality.

The 8th lunar day

The symbol for this day is a Phoenix, which symbolizes eternal rebirth and renewal, because this day is a great time for changes in all areas of your life. Your energy is likely to be high, and you want to do something new and unusual. This is a good time to look for a new job or begin studying something. Any out-of-the-box thinking is welcome, along with shaking things up a bit in order to improve your life.

However, avoid any financial transactions, as you may incur losses.

Avoid aggression. You can share your opinion by presenting well-founded arguments and facts, instead.

The phoenix rises from the ashes, so this is a good time to be careful with electrical appliances and fire in general. The risk of housefires is high.

Avoid any major financial transactions on the eighth day, as you may end up facing a series of complications. You can pay people their salaries, as this is unlikely to be a large sum.

This is a good day for weddings, but only if you and your future spouse are restless, creative souls and hope to achieve personal development through your marriage.

Any cosmetic procedures and plastic surgeries will go well today, as they are related to rebirth and renewal. Surgeons may find that they are true artists on this day!

You can try to change your hairstyle and get a fashionable haircut on this day.

You can trust your dreams seen on this day.

The 9th lunar day

The ninth lunar day is not particularly auspicious, and is even referred to as "Satan's" day. You may be overcome with doubt, suspicions, even depression and conflicts.

Your self-esteem will suffer, so don't overdo things physically, and avoid overeating or abusing alcohol.

This is a negative day for any business deals, travel, or financial transactions.

This is a particularly bad day for any events, so keep your head down at work and avoid any new initiatives.

It is better to avoid getting married on "Satan's" day, as the marriage will not last very long. Avoid sex, as well, but you can take care of your partner, listen them, and support them however they need.

Any cosmetic procedures will not have a lasting effect, and avoid any plastic surgery. A haircut will not turn out as you hoped.

Dreams of this day are usually prophetic.

The 10th lunar day

This is one of the luckiest days of the lunar month. It is symbolized by a spring, mushroom, or phallus. This is a time for starting a new business, learning new things, and creating.

The 10th lunar day is particularly lucky for business. Networking and financial transactions will be a success and bring hope. This is an ideal time for changing jobs, shifting your business tactics, and other renewals.

This is a perfect time for people in creative fields and those working in science, who may come up with incredible ideas that will bring many successful returns.

This is a very successful day for building a family and proposing marriage. This is a good time for celebrations and communication, so plan parties, meet with friends, and plan a romantic date.

One of the symbols for this day is a phallus, so sexual encounters are likely to be particularly satisfying.

The 10th lunar day is the best time to begin repairs, buying furniture, and items for home improvement.

You can exercise vigorously, and cosmetic procedures and plastic surgery will be very effective.

Dreams of this day will not come true.

The 11th lunar day

This is one of the best lunar days, and seen as the pinnacle of the lunar cycle. People are likely to be energetic, enthusiastic, and ready to move forward toward their goals.

The 11th lunar day is very successful for any financial transactions or business deals and meetings.

You might actively make yourself known, approach management to discuss a promotion, or look for a new job. This is an auspicious time for advertising campaigns, performances, and holding meetings.

Any trips planned will be a great success, whether near or far from home.

Romantic relationships are improving, sex is harmonious, and very desired.

Weddings held on this day will be fun, and the marriage will be a source of joy and happiness.

Exercise is a great idea, and you might even beat your own personal record.

This is an ideal time for any cosmetic procedures, but any more serious plastic surgeries might lead to a lot of bruising and swelling.

A haircut will turn out as you had hoped, and you can experiment a bit with your appearance.

You can ignore dreams of this day – usually they do not mean anything.

The 12th lunar day

This day is symbolized by the Grail and a heart. As we move closer to the full moon, our emotions are at their most open. During this time, if you ask someone for something, your request will be heeded. This is a day of faith, goodness, and divine revelations.

For business and financial transactions, this is not the most promising day. However, if you help others on this day, your good deeds are sure to come back to you.

This is a day for reconciliation, so do not try to explain your relationships, as no one is at fault, and it is better to focus on yourself, anyway.

Avoid weddings and sex on this day, but if you want to do what your partner asks, there is no better time.

Many may feel less than confident and cheerful during this day, so take it easy when working out. Avoid overeating, stay hydrated, and avoid alcohol.

The 12th lunar day is not the best for getting married or having sex, but the stars would welcome affection and a kind word.

Avoid getting a haircut, or any plastic surgeries. This is a neutral day for minor cosmetic procedures.

Nearly all dreams will come true.

The 13th lunar day

This day is symbolized by Samsara, the wheel of fate, which is very erratic and capable of moving in any direction. This is why the 13th lunar day is full of contradictions. In Indian traditions, this day is compared to a snake eating its own tail. This is a day for paying off old debts and returning to unfinished business.

Avoid beginning any new business on this day. It is preferable to finish old tasks and proofread your work. Information you receive on this day may not be reliable and must be verified.

It is worth resolving financial problems very carefully, and avoid arguments and conflict.

Do not change jobs on this day or go to a new place for the first time. Do not sit at home alone, though, go see old friends, parents, or older family members.

Minor cosmetic procedures are welcome on this day, but avoid any plastic surgery, as you may experience major swelling and bruising. Avoid any haircuts, too.

As a rule, all dreams will come true.

The 14th lunar day

It's a full moon! The 14th lunar day is one of the happiest, and it is symbolized by the trumpet. Pay attention – you may run into new, much-needed information. Networking will be successful, and you can confidently sign agreements, meet with people, and attend fun gatherings or other leisure activities. This is one of the best days for advertising, performances, and concerts, and those working in creative professions should keep this in mind, as should those who work in politics. Do not sit in place on this day – you need to get out and see others, make new connections, and try to be visible.

This is one of the best days for communication with and making requests from management, as your initiatives will be noticed and welcome. You might talk about a promotion, raise, or something similarly related to professional growth.

Couples will see their relationship is moving along well on this day, and it is also a good day for getting married.

Any sex on this day will be vigorous and memorable for a long time. The full moon is the best time for conceiving a child.

Any cosmetic procedures will be effective, but avoid any major changes to your appearance, as there is a high likelihood of bleeding and bruising. A haircut will turn out well.

Your dreams of this day will be more or less doubtful.

The 15th lunar day

It's a full moon! This day is symbolized by a serpent of fire. This is the energy peak of the entire lunar cycle, and a lot will depend on where you are focusing your energy.

You might face a lot of temptations on this day, for example, you might tell someone else's secret or your own to others, and come to regret it for a long time. The stars suggest exercising restraint in both your words and actions, as the 15th day of the lunar cycle is a day of deception and weaknesses.

This is a very active time, and many people might take unnecessary risks. This is not the best day for signing any agreements or contracts. For any performances, concerts, or advertising, however, this is one of the best days of the month.

You can get married on the 15th day, but only if you know each other well and have carefully considered your partnership, without any hasty decisions. This is also a favorable day for a second marriage.

Your romantic relationship is looking wonderful – you are on cloud 9, writing poetry, and deeply convinced of how right your partner is for you – and they feel the same way. It is important that this does not suddenly lead to an abrupt disappointment.

Avoid getting any haircuts on the 15th day of the month, as you may end up with a headache.

Conservative cosmetic procedures and creams will be very effective, but avoid any injections or plastic surgery today. Bleeding, swelling, and bruising are all but guaranteed.

Dreams on the 15th day nearly always come true.

The 16th lunar day

This day is symbolized by a dove. The full moon is over, and the moon is now in its waning phase. Usually, after the turbulent days of the full moon, people feel a bit under the weather. They are not cheerful, and want to avoid excess worry and give themselves a chance to breathe.

Don't ignore your body's wishes, take it easy with physical activities, and take some time for yourself. You might spend time in nature, in the forest, or at a country home.

The 16th day of the lunar month is a time for moderation in all areas – your behavior, eating, and even in your clothes. If you overate during the full moon period, now is the time to diet a bit or at least avoid fatty foods and meat.

This is not a promising day for resolving any financial matters. Keep your documents in order and get ready for any future meetings, instead. If you help a loved one, your good deed will come back 100 times over.

Avoid getting married today, as well as sex.

Cosmetic procedures are likely to be a success, especially if they are related to cleansing your skin, but it is best to avoid any plastic surgery or injections. Your body is not ready to accept them. A haircut will turn out as you hoped.

Any dreams are likely to come true, but that also depends on a correct interpretation.

The 17th lunar day

This day is represented by a vine and bell. It is a happy day and both successful and fun-filled. It is also a good time for negotiations, concluding small business deals, shaking up staffing, and creativity. However, you should keep in mind that the 17th day is only favorable for minor business, and you should avoid starting any major events.

Avoid any major financial transactions on this day. Do not give anyone money as a loan or borrow anything yourself, either.

Any travel, whether for business or pleasure, is likely to be a success.

The 17th day is a great time to get married, and an ideal day for dates. Any sexual encounters will bring you happiness and joy.

Avoid getting your hair cut on this day, but cosmetic procedures and plastic surgery will be a success. Women will look better than usual.

Your dreams are likely to come true in three days.

The 18th lunar day

This day is represented by a mirror. It is a difficult, and generally unpromising day, too. Just as the mirror reflects our imperfections back to us, we need to remember that moderation and modesty are key.

The 18th day is not a favorable time for any business meetings or financial transactions. You can, however work on jobs you already began. It is, however, a positive day for those who work in research or the creative fields.

Your motto of the day is to keep a cool head when it comes to your opportunities and the opportunities of those around you. This is relevant for both work and romantic relationships. It is not a good time to criticize others – any conflicts or arguments may lead to lasting consequences, which you do not need.

Avoid getting married on this day, as well as sexual encounters, which are likely to be disappointing. It is a good time to take a trip together, which will only be good for your relationship.

Avoid getting your hair cut, though this is a relatively neutral day for a haircut, which might turn out well, and though it will not exceed your expectations, it will also not leave you upset. Avoid any plastic surgeries.

Dreams on this day will come true.

The 19th lunar day

This is a very difficult day and it is represented by a spider. The energy is complicated, if not outright dangerous. Don't panic or get depressed, though – this is a test of your strength, and if you are able to hold onto all you have achieved. This is relevant for both work and love. On the 19th day, you should avoid taking any trips.

The energy of the 19th lunar day is very unfavorable for beginning any major projects, and business in general. Work on what you started earlier, get your affairs in order, think over your ideas and emotions, and check to make sure that everything you have done hitherto is living up to your expectations. Do not carry out any financial transactions or take out any loans – do not loan anyone else money, either. Do not ask your managers for anything as they are unlikely to listen to what you have to say, and make judgments instead.

This is a day when you might face outright deception, so do not take any risks and ignore rumors. Do not work on anything related to real estate or legal matters.

This is a very hard time for people with an unbalanced psyche, as they may experience sudden exacerbations or even suicidal ideations.

This is a very unlucky day to get married. Sexual encounters might be disappointing and significantly worsen your relationship.

Avoid any haircuts or cosmetic procedures or surgeries.

Your dreams of this day will come true.

The 20th lunar day

This is also a difficult day, though less so than the 19th. It is represented by an eagle. This is a good time to work on your own development and spiritual growth, by speaking to a psychologist or astrologer.

Avoid pride, anger, arrogance, and envy.

The 20th lunar day is a good time for people who are active and decisive. They will be able to easily overcome any obstacles, flying over them just like an eagle. If you have to overcome your own fears, you will be able to do so – don't limit yourself, and you will see that there is nothing to be afraid of. It is a good day for any financial transactions, signing contracts, and reaching agreements, as well as networking.

The 20th lunar day is a favorable time for those who work in the creative fields, as they will be able to dream up the idea that will open up a whole host of new possibilities. Avoid conflicts – they may ruin your relationship with a lot of people, and it will not be easy to come back from that.

This is a lucky day for getting married, but only if you have been with your partner for several years, now. Sexual encounters will not be particularly joyful, but they also will not cause you any problems.

Avoid getting your hair cut, but you can certainly get it styled. The 20th lunar day is a good day for those who are looking to lose weight. You will be able to do so quickly, and it will be easy for you to follow a diet.

Cosmetic procedures will be a success, as will any plastic surgeries.

Pay attention to dreams of this day as they are likely to come true.

The 21st lunar day

This is one of the most successful days of the lunar month, and it is symbolized by a herd of horses – imagine energy, strength, speed, and bravery. Everything you think up will happen quickly, and you will be able to easily overcome obstacles. A mare is not only brave but also an honest animal, so you will only experience this luck if you remember that honesty is always the best policy.

This is also a favorable day for business. Reaching new agreements and signing contracts, or dealing with foreign partners – it is all likely to be a success. Any financial issues will be resolved successfully.

Those in the creative world will be able to show off their talent and be recognized for their work. Anyone involved in the performing arts can expect success, luck, and recognition. A galloping herd of horses moves quickly, so you might transition to a new job, move to a new apartment, or go on a business trip or travel with your better half.

The 21st lunar day is one of the best to get married or have a sexual encounter.

This is a great time for athletes, hunters, and anyone who likes adventurous activities.

But for criminals and thieves, this is not a lucky or happy day – they will quickly be brought to justice.

Any haircuts or cosmetic procedures are likely to be a huge success and bring both beauty and happiness. You will recover quickly after any surgeries, perhaps without any swelling or bruising at all.

Dreams tend to not be reliable.

The 22nd lunar day

This day will be strange and contradictory. It is symbolized by the elephant Ganesha. According to Indian mythology, Ganesha is the patron saint of hidden knowledge. so this is a favorable day for anyone who is trying to learn more about the world and ready to find the truth, though this is often seen as a hopeless endeavor. This is a day for philosophers and wisemen and women. However, it is an inauspicious day for business, and unlikely to lead to resolving financial issues, signing contracts, agreements, or beginning new projects. You can expect trouble at work.

For creative people, and new employees, this is a successful day.

This is a good day for apologies and reconciliation.

Avoid getting married, though you can feel free to engage in sexual encounters.

For haircuts and cosmetic procedures, this is a fantastic day. Surgeries will also turn out, as long as the moon is not in Scorpio.

Dreams will come true.

The 23rd lunar day

This is a challenging day represented by a crocodile, which is a very aggressive animal. This is a day of strong energy, but it is also adventurous and tough. Your main task is to focus your energy in the right direction. There may be accidents, arguments, conflicts, fights, and violence, which is why it is important to strive for balance and calm.

Keep a close eye on your surroundings – there may be traitors or people who do not wish you well, so be careful.

However, this is still a favorable day for business – many problems will be resolved successfully. You are able to sign contracts and receive credit successfully, as long as you remain active and decisive in what you do.

This is not a day for changing jobs or working on real estate transactions or legal proceedings. This is not a favorable day for traveling, no matter how near or far you plan on going.

This is not a promising day to get married – things may end in conflict, if not an all-out brawl.

Sexual relations are not off the table, as long as the couple trusts one another.

Haircuts or cosmetic procedures will not turn out as you had hoped, so avoid them.

Dreams during this lunar day usually mean something opposite of what awaits you, so you can disregard them.

The 24ᵗʰ lunar day

This is a neutral, calm day that is symbolized by a bear. It is favorable for forgiveness and reconciliation.

This is also a good day for learning new things, reading, self-development, and taking time to relax in nature.

This is a great day for any type of financial activity, conferences, academic meetings, and faraway travel.

The 24ᵗʰ lunar day is a good time for love and getting married, as any marriage will be strong and lasting.

Cosmetic procedures and plastic surgery will be a success, and you can expect a speedy recovery.

Avoid getting a haircut on this day, however, as your hair will likely thin and grow back slowly.

Dreams of this lunar day are usually connected with your personal life.

The 25th lunar day

This is still another quiet day, symbolized by a turtle.

Just like a turtle, this is not a day to rush, and it is best to sit down and take stock of your life. This is a good time for resolving any personal problems, as the moon's energy makes it possible for you to calm down and find the right path.

This is also not a bad day for business. It is believed that any business you begin on this day is sure to be a success. This is especially the case for trade and any monetary activities.

The 25th lunar day is not a good day to get married, especially if the couple is very young.

This is a neutral day for sexual encounters, as the moon is waning, energy is low, so the decision is yours.

Avoid any cosmetic procedures, except those for cleansing your skin. This is not a favorable day for haircuts or plastic surgery – unless the moon is in Libra or Leo.

You can have a prophetic dream on this day.

The 26th lunar day

The 26th lunar day is full of contradictions and complicated. It is represented by a toad.

It is not time to start or take on something new, as nothing good will come of it. Avoid any major purchases, as you will later come to see that your money was wasted. The best thing you can do on this day is stay at home and watch a good movie or read a good book.

Avoid traveling on this day, as it may not turn out well.

The 26th lunar day is a negative day for any business negotiations and starting new businesses. Do not complete any business deals or financial transactions. Your colleagues may be arguing, and your managers may be dissatisfied. But if you have decided to leave your job, there is no better time to do so.

This is not a good day to get married, as both partners' expectations may fall flat, and they will soon be disappointed.

The waning moon carries a negative charge, so avoid any haircuts and surgeries, though you can get cosmetic procedures if they are relatively minor.

Your dreams will come true.

The 27th lunar day

The 27th lunar day is one of the best days of the month, and it is represented by a ship. You can boldly start any new business, which is sure to be promising. This is a great day for students, teachers, and learning new things. Any information that comes to you on this day may be extremely valuable and useful to you.

The 27th day is good for communication and travel, whether near or far from home, and no matter whether it is for work or pleasure.

This is also a good day for any professional activities or financial transactions. If there are people around you who need help, you must support them, as your good deeds will come back 100-fold.

Romantic dates will go well, though any weddings should be quiet and subdued. This is a particularly good day for older couples or second marriages.

The waning moon means that hair will grow back very slowly, but in general, you can expect a haircut to turn out well. This is a great day for plastic surgery or cosmetic procedures, as the results will be pleasing, and you will have a speedy recovery, without any bruising or swelling, most of the time.

However, beware if the moon is in Scorpio on this day – that is not a good omen for any plastic surgery.

Do not pay any attention to dreams on this day.

The 28th lunar day

This is another favorable day in the waning moon cycle, and it is represented by a lotus. This is a day of wisdom and spiritual awakening. If possible, spend part of the day in nature. It is important to take stock of the last month and decide what you need to do during its two remaining days.

This is a good time for any career development, changing jobs, conducting business, decision-making, and signing agreements, as well as going on a trip. You might conclude any business deal, hold negotiations, work with money and securities.

This is also a good day for any repairs or improvements around your home or apartment.

Anyweddingstodayshouldbesubduedandmodest,andrestrictedtofamily members only. A loud, raucous wedding might not turn out very well.

Your hair will grow slowly, but any haircuts will turn out very elegant and stylish. Cosmetic procedures and surgeries are not contraindicated. You will recover quickly with little bruising and swelling.

Do not take any dreams too seriously.

The 29th lunar day

This is one of the most difficult days of the lunar month, and it is considered a Satanic day, unlucky for everyone and everything. It is symbolized by an octopus.

This is a dark day, and many will feel melancholy, depression, and a desire to simply be left alone. This is a day full of conflict and injuries, so be careful everywhere and with everyone. If you can, avoid any travel, and be particularly careful when handling any sharp objects. Do not engage in any business negotiations, sign any contracts, or take part in any networking.

Astrologers believe that anything you start on this day will completely fall apart. For once and for all, get rid of things that are impeding you from living your life. This is a good time to avoid people who you do find unpleasant.

This is also a time for fasting and limitations for everyone. Do not hold any celebrations, weddings, or have sexual relations – these events may not turn out as you hoped, and instead bring you nothing but suffering and strife.

Avoid getting a haircut, as well, as it will not make you look more beautiful and your hair will come back lifeless and dull. Cosmetic procedures can go ahead, but avoid any surgeries.

Dreams are likely to be true.

The 30th lunar day

There is not always a 30th lunar day, as some lunar months have only 29 days. This day is represented by a swan. The 30th lunar day is usually very short, and sometimes, it lasts less than an hour. This is a time for forgiveness and calm.

You might take stock of the last month, while also avoiding anything you do not need around you. Pay back loans, make donations, reconcile with those who recently offended you, and stop speaking to people who cause you suffering.

This is a good time for tying up loose ends, and many astrologers believe that it is also a good day to start new business.

However, avoid celebrations or weddings on this day. Spouses will either not live long, or they will quickly grow apart.

Do not get a haircut on this day, though cosmetic procedures are possible, as long as you avoid any surgeries.

Dreams promise happiness and should come true.

A Guide to Zodiac Compatibility

Often, when we meet a person, we get a feeling that they are good and we take an instant liking to them. Another person, however, gives us immediate feelings of distrust, fear and hostility. Is there an astrological reason why people say that 'the first impression is the most accurate'? How can we detect those who will bring us nothing but trouble and unhappiness?

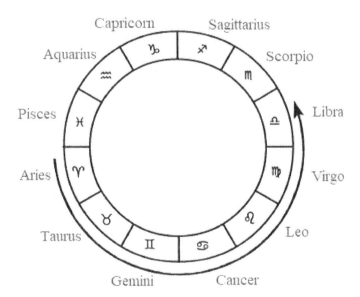

Without going too deeply into astrological subtleties unfamiliar to some readers, it is possible to determine the traits according to which friendship, love or business relationships will develop.

Let's begin with problematic relationships - our most difficult are with our **8th sign**. For example, for Aries the 8th sign is Scorpio, for Taurus it is Sagittarius and so on. Finding your 8th sign is easy; assume your own sign to be first (see above Figure) and then move eight signs counter clockwise around the Zodiac circle. This is also how the other signs (fourth, ninth and so on) that we mention are to be found.

Ancient astrologers variously referred to the 8th sign as the symbol of death, of destruction, of fated love or unfathomable attraction. In astrological terms, this pair is called 'master and slave' or 'boa constrictor and rabbit', with the role of 'master' or 'boa constrictor' being played by our 8th sign.

This relationship is especially difficult for politicians and business people.

We can take the example of a recent political confrontation in the USA. Hilary Clinton is a Scorpio while Donald Trump is a Gemini - her 8th sign. Even though many were certain that Clinton would be elected President, she lost.

To take another example, Hitler was a Taurus and his opponents – Stalin and Churchill - were both of his 8th sign, Sagittarius. The result of their confrontation is well known. Interestingly, the Russian Marshals who dealt crushing military blows to Hitler and so helped end the Third Reich - Konstantin Rokossovsky and Georgy Zhukov - were also Sagittarian, Hitler's 8th sign.

In another historical illustration, Lenin was also a Taurus. Stalin was of Lenin's 8th sign and was ultimately responsible for the downfall and possibly death of his one-time comrade-in-arms.

Business ties with those of our 8th sign are hazardous as they ultimately lead to stress and loss; both financial and moral. So, do not tangle with your 8th sign and never fight with it - your chances of winning are remote!

Such relationships are very interesting in terms of love and romance, however. We are magnetically attracted to our 8th sign and even though it may be very intense physically, it is very difficult for family life;

'Feeling bad when together, feeling worse when apart'.

As an example, let us take the famous lovers - George Sand who was Cancer and Alfred de Musset who was Sagittarius. Cancer is the 8th sign for Sagittarius, and the story of their crazy two-year love affair was the subject of much attention throughout France. Critics and writers were divided into 'Mussulist' and 'Sandist' camps; they debated fiercely about who was to blame for the sad ending to their love story - him or her. It's hard to imagine the energy needed to captivate the public for so long, but that energy was destructive for the couple. Passion raged in their hearts, but neither of them was able to comprehend their situation.

Georges Sand wrote to Musset, "*I ✦on't love you anymore, an✦ I will always a✦ore you. I ✦on't want you anymore, an✦ I can't ✦o without you. It seems that nothing but a heavenly lightning strike can heal me by ✦estroying me. Goo✦-bye! Stay or go, but ✦on't say that I am not suffering. This is the only thing that can make me suffer even more, my love, my life, my bloo✦! Go away, but kill me, leaving.*" Musset replied only in brief, but its power surpassed Sand's tirade, "*When you embrace✦ me, I felt something that is still bothering me, making it impossible for me to approach another woman.*" These two people loved each other passionately and for two years lived together in a powder keg of passion, hatred and treachery.

When someone enters into a romantic liaison with their 8th sign, there will be no peace; indeed, these relationships are very attractive to those who enjoy the edgy, the borderline and, in the Dostoevsky style, the melodramatic. The first to lose interest in the relationship is, as a rule, the 8th sign.

If, by turn of fate, our child is born under our 8th sign, they will be very different from us and, in some ways, not live up to our expectations. It may be best to let them choose their own path.

In business and political relationships, the combination with our **12th sign** is also a complicated one.

We can take two political examples. Angela Merkel is a Cancer while Donald Trump is a Gemini - her 12th sign. This is why their relations are strained and complicated and we can even perhaps assume that the American president will achieve his political goals at her expense. Boris Yeltsin (Aquarius) was the 12th sign to Mikhail Gorbachev (Pisces) and it was Yeltsin who managed to dethrone the champion of Perestroika.

Even ancient astrologers noticed that our relationships with our 12th signs can never develop evenly; it is one of the most curious and problematic combinations. They are our hidden enemies and they seem to be digging a hole for us; they ingratiate themselves with us, discover our innermost secrets. As a result, we become bewildered and make mistakes when we deal with them. Among the Roman emperors murdered by members of their entourage, there was an interesting pattern - all the murderers were the 12th sign of the murdered.

We can also see this pernicious effect in Russian history: the German princess Alexandra (Gemini) married the last Russian Tsar Nicholas II (Taurus) - he was her 12th sign and brought her a tragic death. The wicked genius Grigory Rasputin (Cancer) made friends with Tsarina Alexandra, who was his 12th sign, and was murdered as a result of their odd friendship. The weakness of Nicholas II was exposed, and his authority reduced after the death of the economic and social reformer Pyotr Stolypin, who was his 12th sign. Thus, we see a chain of people whose downfall was brought about by their 12th sign.

So, it makes sense to be cautious of your 12th sign, especially if you have business ties. Usually, these people know much more about us than we want them to and they will often reveal our secrets for personal gain if it suits them. However, the outset of these relationships is, as a rule, quite normal - sometimes the two people will be friends, but sooner or later one will betray the other one or divulge a secret; inadvertently or not.

In terms of romantic relationships, our 12th sign is gentle, they take care of us and are tender towards us. They know our weaknesses well but accept them with understanding. It is they who guide us, although sometimes almost imperceptibly. Sexual attraction is usually strong.

For example, Meghan Markle is a Leo, the 12th sign for Prince Harry, who is a Virgo. Despite Queen Elizabeth II being lukewarm about the match, Harry's love was so strong that they did marry.

If a child is our 12th sign, it later becomes clear that they know all our secrets, even those that they are not supposed to know. It is very difficult to control them as they do everything in their own way.

Relations with our **7th sign** are also interesting. They are like our opposite; they have something to learn from us while we, in turn, have something to learn from them. This combination, in business and personal relationships, can be very positive and stimulating provided that both partners are quite intelligent and have high moral standards but if not, constant misunderstandings and challenges follow. Marriage or co-operation with the 7th sign can only exist as the union of two fully-fledged individuals and in this case love, significant business achievements and social success are possible.

However, the combination can be not only interesting, but also quite complicated.

An example is Angelina Jolie, a Gemini, and Brad Pitt, a Sagittarius. This is a typical bond with a 7th sign - it's lively and interesting, but rather stressful. Although such a couple may quarrel and even part from time to time, never do they lose interest in each other.

This may be why this combination is more stable in middle-age when there is an understanding of the true nature of marriage and partnership. In global, political terms, this suggests a state of eternal tension - a cold war - for example between Yeltsin (Aquarius) and Bill Clinton (Leo).

Relations with our **9th sign** are very good; they are our teacher and advisor - one who reveals things we are unaware of and our relationships with them very often involve travel or re-location. The combination can lead to spiritual growth and can be beneficial in terms of business.

Although, for example, Trump and Putin are political opponents, they can come to an understanding and even feel a certain sympathy for each other because Putin is a Libra while Trump is a Gemini, his 9th sign.

This union is also quite harmonious for conjugal and romantic relationships.

We treat our **3ʳᵈ sign** somewhat condescendingly. They are like our younger siblings; we teach them and expect them to listen attentively. Our younger brothers and sisters are more often than not born under this sign. In terms of personal and sexual relationships, the union is not very inspiring and can end quickly, although this is not always the case. In terms of business, it is fairly average as it often connects partners from different cities or countries.

We treat our **5ᵗʰ sign** as a child and we must take care of them accordingly. The combination is not very good for business, however, since our 5ᵗʰ sign triumphs over us in terms of connections and finances, and thereby gives us very little in return save for love or sympathy. However, they are very good for family and romantic relationships, especially if the 5ᵗʰ sign is female. If a child is born as a 5ᵗʰ sign to their parents, their relationship will be a mutually smooth, loving and understanding one that lasts a lifetime.

Our **10ᵗʰ sign** is a born leader. Depending on the spiritual level of those involved, both pleasant and tense relations are possible; the relationship is often mutually beneficial in the good times but mutually disruptive in the bad times. In family relations, our 10ᵗʰ sign always tries to lead and will do so according to their intelligence and upbringing.

Our **4ᵗʰ sign** protects our home and can act as a sponsor to strengthen our financial or moral positions. Their advice should be heeded in all cases as it can be very effective, albeit very unobtrusive. If a woman takes this role, the relationship can be long and romantic, since all the spouse's wishes are usually met one way or another. Sometimes, such couples achieve great social success; for instance, Hilary Clinton, a Scorpio is the 4ᵗʰ sign to Bill Clinton, a Leo. On the other hand, if the husband is the 4ᵗʰ sign for his wife, he tends to be henpecked. There is often a strong sexual attraction. Our 4ᵗʰ sign can improve our living conditions and care for us in a parental way. If a child is our 4ᵗʰ sign, they are close to us and support us affectionately.

Relations with our **11th sign** are often either friendly or patronizing; we treat them reverently, while they treat us with friendly condescension. Sometimes, these relationships develop in an 'older brother' or 'high-ranking friend' sense; indeed, older brothers and sisters are often our 11th sign. In terms of personal and sexual relationships, our 11th sign is always inclined to enslave us. This tendency is most clearly manifested in such alliances as Capricorn and Pisces or Leo and Libra. A child who is the 11th sign to their parents will achieve greater success than their parents, but this will only make the parents proud.

Our **2nd sign** should bring us financial or other benefits; we receive a lot from them in both our business and our family life. In married couples, the 2nd sign usually looks after the financial situation for the benefit of the family. Sexual attraction is strong.

Our **6th sign** is our 'slave'; we always benefit from working with them and it's very difficult for them to escape our influence. In the event of hostility, especially if they have provoked the conflict, they receive a powerful retaliatory strike. In personal relations, we can almost destroy them by making them dance to our tune. For example, if a husband doesn't allow his wife to work or there are other adverse family circumstances, she gradually becomes lost as an individual despite being surrounded by care. This is the best-case scenario; worse outcomes are possible. Our 6th sign has a strong sexual attraction to us because we are the fatal 8th sign for them; we cool down quickly, however, and often make all kinds of demands. If the relationship with our 6th sign is a long one, there is a danger that routine, boredom and stagnation will ultimately destroy the relationship. A child born under our 6th sign needs particularly careful handling as they can feel fear or embarrassment when communicating with us. Their health often needs increased attention and we should also remember that they are very different from us emotionally.

Finally, we turn to relations with **our own sign**. Scorpio with Scorpio and Cancer with Cancer get along well, but in most other cases, however, our own sign is of little interest to us as it has a similar energy. Sometimes, this relationship can develop as a rivalry, either in business or in love.

There is another interesting detail - we are often attracted to one particular sign. For example, a man's wife and mistress often have the same sign. If there is confrontation between the two, the stronger character displaces the weaker one. As an example, Prince Charles is a Scorpio, while both Princess Diana and Camilla Parker Bowles were born under the sign of Cancer. Camilla was the more assertive and became dominant.

Of course, in order to draw any definitive conclusions, we need an individually prepared horoscope, but the above always, one way or another, manifests itself.

Love Description of Zodiac Signs

We know that human sexual behavior has been studied at length. Entire libraries have been written about it, with the aim of helping us understand ourselves and our partners. But is that even possible? It may not be; no matter how smart we are, when it comes to love and sex, there is always an infinite amount to learn. But we have to strive for perfection, and astrology, with its millennia of research, twelve astrological types, and twelve zodiac signs, may hold the key. Below, you will find a brief and accurate description of each zodiac sign's characteristics in love, for both men and women.

Men

ARIES

Aries men are not particularly deep or wise, but they make up for it in sincerity and loyalty. They are active, even aggressive lovers, but a hopeless romantic may be lurking just below the surface. Aries are often monogamous and chivalrous men, for whom there is only one woman (of course, in her absence, they can sleep around with no remorse). If the object of your affection is an Aries, be sure to give him a lot of sex, and remember that for an Aries, when it comes to sex, anything goes. Aries cannot stand women who are negative or disheveled. They need someone energetic, lively, and to feel exciting feelings of romance.

The best partner for an Aries is Cancer, Sagittarius, or Leo. Aquarius can also be a good match, but the relationship will be rather friendly in nature. Partnering with a Scorpio or Taurus will be difficult, but they can be stimulating lovers for an Aries. Virgos are good business contacts, but a poor match as lovers or spouses.

TAURUS

A typical Taurean man is warm, friendly, gentle, and passionate, even if he doesn't always show it. He is utterly captivated by the beauty of the female body, and can find inspiration in any woman. A Taurus has such excess physical and sexual prowess, that to him, sex is a way to relax and calm down. He is the most passionate and emotional lover of the Zodiac, but he expects his partner to take the initiative, and if she doesn't, he will easily find someone else. Taureans rarely divorce, and are true to the end – if not sexually, at least spiritually. They are secretive, keep their cards close, and may have secret lovers. If a Taurus does not feel a deep emotional connection with someone, he won't be shy to ask her friends for their number. He prefers a voluptuous figure over an athletic or skinny woman.

The best partners for a Taurus are Cancer, Virgo, Pisces, or Scorpio. Sagittarius can show a Taurus real delights in both body and spirit, but they are unlikely to make it down the aisle. They can have an interesting relationship with an Aquarius – these signs are very different, but sometimes can spend their lives together. They might initially feel attracted to an Aries, before rejecting her.

GEMINI

The typical Gemini man is easygoing and polite. He is calm, collected, and analytical. For a Gemini, passion is closely linked to intellect, to the point that they will try to find an explanation for their actions before carrying them out. But passion cannot be explained, which scares a Gemini, and they begin jumping from one extreme to the other. This is why you will find more bigamists among Geminis than any other sign of the Zodiac. Sometimes, Gemini men even have two families, or divorce and marry several times throughout the course of their lives. This may be because they simply can't let new and interesting experiences pass them by. A Gemini's wife or lover needs to be smart, quick, and always looking ahead. If she isn't, he will find a new object for his affection.

Aquarians, Libras, and Aries make good partners for a Gemini. A Sagittarius can be fascinating for him, but they will not marry before he reaches middle age, as both partners will be fickle while they are younger. A Gemini and Scorpio are likely to be a difficult match, and the Gemini will try to wriggle out of the Scorpio's tight embrace. A Taurus will be an exciting sex partner, but their partnership won't be for long, and the Taurus is often at fault.

CANCER

Cancers tend to be deep, emotional individuals, who are both sensitive and highly sexual. Their charm is almost mystical, and they know how to use it. Cancers may be the most promiscuous sign of the Zodiac, and open to absolutely anything in bed. Younger Cancers look for women who are more mature, as they are skilled lovers. As they age, they look for someone young enough to be their own daughter, and delight in taking on the role of a teacher. Cancers are devoted to building a family and an inviting home, but once they achieve that goal, they are likely to have a wandering eye. They will not seek moral justification, as they sincerely believe it is simply something everyone does. Their charm works in such a way that women are deeply convinced they are the most important love in a Cancer's life, and that circumstances are the only thing preventing them from being together. Remember that a Cancer man is a master manipulator, and will not be yours unless he is sure you have throngs of admirers. He loves feminine curves, and is turned on by exquisite fragrances. Cancers don't end things with old lovers, and often go back for a visit after a breakup. Another type of Cancer is rarer – a faithful friend, and up for anything in order to provide for his wife and children. He is patriotic and a responsible worker.

Scorpios, Pisces, and other Cancers are a good match. A Taurus can make for a lasting relationship, as both signs place great value on family and are able to get along with one another. A Sagittarius will result in fights and blowouts from the very beginning, followed by conflicts and breakups. The Sagittarius will suffer the most. Marriage to an Aries isn't off the table, but it won't last very long.

LEO

A typical Leo is handsome, proud, and vain, with a need to be the center of attention at all times. They often pretend to be virtuous, until they are able to actually master it. They crave flattery, and prefer women who comply and cater to them. Leos demand unconditional obedience, and constant approval. When a Leo is in love, he is fairly sexual, and capable of being devoted and faithful. Cheap love affairs are not his thing, and Leos are highly aware of how expensive it is to divorce. They make excellent fathers. A Leo's partner needs to look polished and well-dressed, and he will not tolerate either frumpiness or nerds.

Aries, Sagittarius, and Gemini make for good matches. Leos are often very beguiling to Libras; this is the most infamous astrological "master-slave" pairing. Leos are also inexplicably drawn to Pisces – this is the only sign capable of taming them. A Leo and Virgo will face a host of problems sooner or later, and they might be material in nature. The Virgo will attempt to conquer him, and if she does, a breakup is inevitable.

VIRGO

Virgo is a highly intellectual sign, who likes to take a step back and spend his time studying the big picture. But love inherently does not lend itself to analysis, and this can leave Virgos feeling perplexed. While Virgo is taking his time, studying the object of his affection, someone else will swoop in and take her away, leaving him bitterly disappointed. Perhaps for that reason, Virgos tend to marry late, but once they are married, they remain true, and hardly ever initiate divorce. In bed, they are modest and reserved, as they see sex as some sort of quirk of nature, designed solely for procreation. Most Virgos have a gifted sense of taste, hearing, and smell. They cannot tolerate pungent odors and can be squeamish; they believe their partners should always take pains to be very clean. Virgos usually hate over-the-top expressions of love, and are immune to sex as a mean s of control. Many Virgos are stingy and more appropriate as husbands than lovers. Male Virgos tend to be monogamous, though if they are unhappy or disappointed with their partner, they may begin to look for comfort elsewhere and often give in to drunkenness.

Taurus, Capricorn, and Scorpio make the best partners for a Virgo. They may feel inexplicable attraction for Aquarians. They will form friendships with Aries, but rarely will this couple make it down the aisle. With Leos, be careful – this sign is best as a lover, not a spouse.

LIBRA

Libra is a very complex, wishy-washy sign. They are constantly seeking perfection, which often leaves them in discord with the reality around them. Libra men are elegant and refined, and expect no less from their partner. Many Libras treat their partners like a beautiful work of art, and have trouble holding onto the object of their affection. They view love itself as a very abstract concept, and can get tired of the physical aspect of their relationship. They are much more drawn to intrigue and the chase- dreams, candlelit evenings, and other symbols of romance. A high percentage of Libra men are gay, and they view sex with other men as the more elite option. Even when Libras are unhappy in their marriages, they never divorce willingly. Their wives might leave them, however, or they might be taken away by a more decisive partner.

Aquarius and Gemini make the best matches for Libras. Libra can also easily control an independent Sagittarius, and can easily fall under the influence of a powerful and determined Leo, before putting all his strength and effort into breaking free. Relationships with Scorpios are difficult; they may become lovers, but will rarely marry.

SCORPIO

Though it is common to perceive Scorpios as incredibly sexual, they are, in fact, very unassuming, and never brag about their exploits. They will, however, be faithful and devoted to the right woman. The Scorpio man is taciturn, and you can't expect any tender words from him, but he will defend those he loves to the very end. Despite his outward control, Scorpio is very emotional; he needs and craves love, and is willing to fight for it. Scorpios are incredible lovers, and rather than leaving them tired, sex leaves them feeling energized. They are always sexy, even if they aren't particularly handsome. They are unconcerned with the ceremony of wooing you, and more focused on the act of love itself.

Expressive Cancers and gentle, amenable Pisces make the best partners. A Scorpio might also fall under the spell of a Virgo, who is adept at taking the lead. Sparks might fly between two Scorpios, or with a Taurus, who is perfect for a Scorpio in bed. Relationships with Libras, Sagittarians, and Aries are difficult.

SAGITTARIUS

Sagittarian men are lucky, curious, and gregarious. Younger Sagittarians are romantic, passionate, and burning with desire to experience every type of love. Sagittarius is a very idealistic sign, and in that search for perfection, they tend to flit from one partner to another, eventually forgetting what they were even looking for in the first place. A negative Sagittarius might have two or three relationships going on at once, assigning each partner a different day of the week. On the other hand, a positive Sagittarius will channel his powerful sexual energy into creativity, and take his career to new heights. Generally speaking, after multiple relationships and divorces, the Sagittarian man will conclude that his ideal marriage is one where his partner is willing to look the other way.

Aries and Leo make the best matches for a Sagittarius. He might fall under the spell of a Cancer, but would not be happy being married to her. Gemini can be very intriguing, but will only make for a happy marriage after middle age, when both partners are older and wiser. Younger Sagittarians often marry Aquarian women, but things quickly fall apart. Scorpios can make for an interesting relationship, but if the Sagittarius fails to comply, divorce is inevitable.

CAPRICORN

Practical, reserved Capricorn is one of the least sexual signs of the Zodiac. He views sex as an idle way to pass the time, and something he can live without, until he wants to start a family. He tends to marry late, and almost never divorces. Young Capricorns are prone to suppressing their sexual desires, and only discover them later in life, when they have already achieved everything a real man needs – a career and money. We'll be frank – Capricorn is not the best lover, but he can compensate by being caring, attentive, and showering you with valuable gifts. Ever cautious, Capricorn loves to schedule his sexual relationships, and this is something partners will just have to accept. Women should understand that Capricorn needs some help relaxing – perhaps with alcohol. They prefer inconspicuous, unassuming women, and run away from a fashion plate.

The best partners for a Capricorn are Virgo, Taurus, or Scorpio. Cancers might catch his attention, and if they marry, it is likely to be for life. Capricorn is able to easily dominate Pisces, and Pisces-Capricorn is a well-known "slave and master" combination. Relationships with Leos tend to be erratic, and they are unlikely to wed. Aries might make for a cozy family at first, but things will cool off quickly, and often, the marriage only lasts as long as Capricorn is unwilling to make a change in his life.

AQUARIUS

Aquarian men are mercurial, and often come off as peculiar, unusual, or aloof, and detached. Aquarians are turned on by anything novel or strange, and they are constantly looking for new and interesting people. They are stimulated by having a variety of sexual partners, but they consider this to simply be normal life, rather than sexually immoral. Aquarians are unique – they are more abstract than realistic, and can be cold and incomprehensible, even in close relationships. Once an Aquarius gets married, he will try to remain within the realm of decency, but often fails. An Aquarian's partners need uncommon patience, as nothing they do can restrain him. Occasionally, one might encounter another kind of Aquarius – a responsible, hard worker, and exemplary family man.

The best matches for an Aquarius are female fellow Aquarians, Libras, and Sagittarians. When Aquarius seeks out yet another affair, he is not choosy, and will be happy with anyone.

PISCES

Pisces is the most eccentric sign of the Zodiac. This is reflected in his romantic tendencies and sex life. Pisces men become very dependent on those with whom they have a close relationship. Paradoxically, they are simultaneously crafty and childlike when it comes to playing games, and they are easily deceived. As a double bodied sign, Pisces rarely marry just once, as they are very sexual, easily fall in love, and are constantly seeking their ideal. Pisces are very warm people, who love to take care of others and are inclined toward "slave-master" relationships, in which they are the submissive partner. But after catering to so many lovers, Pisces will remain elusive. They are impossible to figure out ahead of time – today, they might be declaring their love for you, but tomorrow, they may disappear – possibly forever! To a Pisces, love is a fantasy, illusion, and dream, and they might spend their whole lives in pursuit of it. Pisces who are unhappy in love are vulnerable to alcoholism or drug addiction.

Cancer and Scorpio make the best partners for a Pisces. He is also easily dominated by Capricorn and Libra, but in turn will conquer even a queen-like Leo. Often, they are fascinated by Geminis – if they marry, it will last a long time, but likely not forever. Relationships with Aries and Sagittarians are erratic, though initially, things can seem almost perfect.

Women

ARIES

Aries women are leaders. They are decisive, bold, and very protective. An Aries can take initiative and is not afraid to make the first move. Her ideal man is strong, and someone she can admire. But remember, at the slightest whiff of weakness, she will knock him off his pedestal. She does not like dull, whiny men, and thinks that there is always a way out of any situation. If she loves someone, she will be faithful. Aries women are too honest to try leading a double life. They are possessive, jealous, and not only will they not forgive those who are unfaithful, their revenge may be brutal; they know no limits. If you can handle an Aries, don't try to put her in a cage; it is best to give her a long leash. Periodically give her some space – then she will seek you out herself. She is sexual, and believe that anything goes in bed.

Her best partners are a Sagittarius or Leo. A Libra can make a good match after middle age, once both partners have grown wiser and settled down a bit. Gemini and Aquarius are only good partners during the initial phase, when everything is still new, but soon enough, they will lose interest in each other. Scorpios are good matches in bed, but only suitable as lovers.

TAURUS

Taurean women possess qualities that men often dream about, but rarely find in the flesh – they are soft, charming, practical, and reliable – they are very caring and will support their partner in every way. A Taurus is highly sexual, affectionate, and can show a man how to take pleasure to new heights. She is also strong and intense. If she is in love, she will be faithful. But when love fades away, she might find someone else on the side, though she will still fight to save her marriage, particularly if her husband earns good money. A Taurus will not tolerate a man who is disheveled or disorganized, and anyone dating her needs to always be on his toes. She will expect gifts, and likes being taken to expensive restaurants, concerts, and other events. If you argue, try to make the first peace offering, because a Taurus finds it very hard to do so – she might withdraw and ruminate for a long time. Never air your dirty laundry; solve all your problems one-on-one.

Scorpio, Virgo, Capricorn, and Cancer make the best matches. A relationship with an Aries or Sagittarius would be difficult. There is little attraction between a Taurus and a Leo, and initially Libras can make for a good partner in bed, but things will quickly cool off and fall apart. A Taurus and Aquarius make an interesting match – despite the difference in signs, their relationships are often lasting, and almost lifelong.

GEMINI

Gemini women are social butterflies, outgoing, and they easily make friends, and then break off the friendship, if people do not hold their interest. A Gemini falls in love hard, is very creative, and often fantasizes about the object of her affection. She is uninterested in sex without any attachment, loves to flirt, and, for the most part, is not particularly affectionate. She dreams of a partner who is her friend, lover, and a romantic, all at once. A Gemini has no use for a man who brings nothing to the table intellectually. That is a tall order, so Geminis often divorce and marry several times. Others simply marry later in life. Once you have begun a life together, do not try to keep her inside – she needs to travel, explore, socialize, attend events and go to the theater. She cannot tolerate possessive men, so avoid giving her the third degree, and remember that despite her flirtatious and social nature, she is, in fact, faithful – as long as you keep her interested and she is in love. Astrologists believe that Geminis do not know what they need until age 29 or 30, so it is best to hold off on marriage until then.

Leo and Libra make the best matches. A relationship with a Cancer is likely, though complex, and depends solely on the Cancer's affection. A Gemini and Sagittarius can have an interesting, dynamic relationship, but these are two restless signs, which might only manage to get together after ages 40-45, once they have had enough thrills out of life and learned to be patient. Relationships with a Capricorn are very difficult, and almost never happen. The honeymoon stage can be wonderful with a Scorpio, but each partner will eventually go their own way, before ending things. A Gemini and Pisces union can also be very interesting – they are drawn to each other, and can have a wonderful relationship, but after a while, the cracks start to show and things will fall apart. An Aquarius is also not a bad match, but they will have little sexual chemistry.

CANCER

Cancers can be divided into two opposing groups. The first includes a sweet and gentle creature who is willing to dedicate her life to her husband and children. She is endlessly devoted to her husband, especially if he makes a decent living and remains faithful. She views all men as potential husbands, which means it is dangerous to strike up a relationship with her if your intentions are not serious; she can be anxious and clingy, sensitive and prone to crying. It is better to break things to her gently, rather than directly spitting out the cold, hard truth. She wants a man who can be a provider, though she often earns well herself. She puts money away for a rainy day, and knows how to be thrifty, for the sake of others around her, rather than only for herself. She is an excellent cook and capable of building an inviting home for her loved ones. She is enthusiastic in bed, a wonderful wife, and a caring mother.

The second type of Cancer is neurotic, and capable of creating a living hell for those around her. She believes that the world is her enemy, and manages to constantly find new intrigue and machinations.

Another Cancer, Virgo, Taurus, Scorpio, and Pisces make the best matches. A Cancer can often fall in love with a Gemini, but eventually, things will grow complicated, as she will be exhausted by a Gemini's constant mood swings and cheating. A Cancer and Sagittarius will initially have passionate sex, but things will quickly cool off. A relationship with a Capricorn is a real possibility, but only later in life, as while they are young, they are likely to fight and argue constantly. Cancer can also have a relationship with an Aries, but this will not be easy.

LEO

Leos are usually beautiful or charming, and outwardly sexual. And yet, appearances can be deceiving – they are not actually that interested in sex. Leo women want to be the center of attention and men running after them boosts their self-esteem, but they are more interested in their career, creating something new, and success than sex. They often have high-powered careers and are proud of their own achievements. Their partners need to be strong; if a Leo feels a man is weak, she can carry him herself for a while- before leaving him. It is difficult for her to find a partner for life, as chivalrous knights are a dying breed, and she is not willing to compromise. If you are interested in a Leo, take the initiative, admire her, and remember that even a queen is still a woman. Timid men or tightwads need not apply. Leos like to help others, but they don't need a walking disaster in their life. If they are married and in love, they are usually faithful, and petty gossip isn't their thing. Leo women make excellent mothers, and are ready to give their lives to their children. Their negative traits include vanity and a willingness to lie, in order to make themselves look better.

Sagittarius, Aries, and Libra make the best matches. Leos can also have an interesting relationship with a Virgo, though both partners will weaken each other. Life with a Taurus will lead to endless arguments – both signs are very stubborn, and unwilling to give in. Leos and Pisces are another difficult pair, as she will have to learn to be submissive if she wants to keep him around. A relationship with a Capricorn will work if there is a common denominator, but they will have little sexual chemistry. Life with a Scorpio will be turbulent to say the least, and they will usually break up later in life.

VIRGO

Virgo women are practical, clever, and often duplicitous. Marrying one isn't for everyone. She is a neat freak to the point of annoying those around her. She is also an excellent cook, and strives to ensure her children receive the very best by teaching them everything, and preparing them for a bright future. She is also thrifty – she won't throw money around, and, in fact, won't even give it to her husband. She has no time for rude, macho strongmen, and is suspicious of spendthrifts. She will not be offended if you take her to a cozy and modest café rather than an elegant restaurant. Virgos are masters of intrigue, and manage to outperform every other sign of the Zodiac in this regard. Virgos love to criticize everyone and everything; to listen to them, the entire world is simply a disaster and wrong, and only she is the exception to this rule. Virgos are not believed to be particularly sexual, but there are different variations when it comes to this. Rarely, one finds an open-minded Virgo willing to try anything, and who does it all on a grand scale – but she is rather the exception to this general rule.

The best matches for a Virgo are Cancer, Taurus, and Capricorn. She also can get along well with a Scorpio, but will find conflict with Sagittarius. A Pisces will strike her interest, but they will rarely make it down the aisle. She is often attracted to an Aquarius, but they would drive each other up the wall were they to actually marry. An Aries forces Virgo to see another side of life, but here, she will have to learn to conform and adapt.

LIBRA

Female Libras tend to be beautiful, glamorous, or very charming. They are practical, tactical, rational, though they are adept at hiding these qualities behind their romantic and elegant appearance. Libras are drawn to marriage, and are good at imagining the kind of partner they need. They seek out strong, well-off men and are often more interested in someone's social status and bank account than feelings. The object of their affection needs to be dashing, and have a good reputation in society. Libras love expensive things, jewelry, and finery. If they are feeling down, a beautiful gift will instantly cheer them up. They will not tolerate scandal or conflict, and will spend all their energy trying to keep the peace, or at least the appearance thereof. They do not like to air their dirty laundry, and will only divorce in extreme circumstances. They are always convinced they are right and react to any objections as though they have been insulted. Most Libras are not particularly sexual, except those with Venus or the Moon in Scorpio.

Leos, Geminis, and Aquarians make good matches. Libra women are highly attracted to Aries men - this is a real case of opposites attract. They can get along with a Sagittarius, though he will find that Libras are too proper and calm. Capricorn, Pisces, and Cancer are all difficult matches. Things will begin tumultuously with a Taurus, before each partner goes his or her own way.

SCORPIO

Scorpio women may appear outwardly restrained, but there is much more bubbling below the surface. They are ambitious with high self-esteem, but often wear a mask of unpretentiousness. They are the true power behind the scenes, the one who holds the family together, but never talk about it. Scorpios are strong-willed, resilient, and natural survivors. Often, Scorpios are brutally honest, and expect the same out of those around them. They do not like having to conform, and attempt to get others to adapt to them, as they honestly believe everyone will be better off that way. They are incredibly intuitive, and not easily deceived. They have an excellent memory, and can quickly figure out which of your buttons to push. They are passionate in bed, and their temperament will not diminish with age. When she is sexually frustrated, a Scorpio will throw all of her energy into her career or her loved ones. She is proud, categorical, and "if you don't do it right, don't do it at all" is her motto. Scorpio cannot be fooled, and she will not forgive any cheating. Will she cheat herself? Yes! But it will not break up her family, and she will attempt to keep it a secret. Scorpios are usually attractive to men, even if they are not particularly beautiful. They keep a low profile, though they always figure out their partner, and give them some invisible sign. There is also another, selfish type of Scorpio, who will use others for as long as they need them, before unceremoniously casting them aside.

Taurus is a good match; they will have excellent sexual chemistry and understand each other. Scorpio and Gemini are drawn to each other, but are unlikely to stay together long enough to actually get married. Cancer can be a good partner as well, but Cancers are possessive, while Scorpios do not like others meddling in their affairs, though they can later resolve their arguments in bed. Scorpio and Leo are often found together, but their relationship can also be very complicated. Leos are animated and chipper, while Scorpios, who are much deeper and more stubborn, see Leos as not particularly serious or reliable. One good example of this is Bill (a Leo) and Hillary (a Scorpio) Clinton. Virgo can also make a good partner, but when Scorpio seemingly lacks emotions, he will look for them elsewhere. Relationships with Lira are strange and very rare. Scorpio sees Libra as too insecure, and Libra does not appreciate Scorpio's rigidity. Two Scorpios together make an excellent marriage! Sagittarius and Scorpio are unlikely to get together, as she will think he is shallow and rude. If they do manage to get married, Scorpio's drive and persistence is the only thing that will make the marriage last. Capricorn is also not a bad match, and while Scorpio finds Aquarius attractive, they will rarely get married, as they are simply speaking different languages! Things are alright with a Pisces, as both signs are emotional, and Pisces can let Scorpio take the lead when necessary.

SAGITTARIUS

Sagittarius women are usually charming, bubbly, energetic, and have the gift of gab. They are kind, sincere, and love people. They are also straightforward, fair, and very ambitious, occasionally to the point of irritating those around them. But telling them something is easier than not telling them, and they often manage to win over their enemies. Sagittarius tends to have excellent intuition, and she loves to both learn and teach others. She is a natural leader, and loves taking charge at work and at home. Many Sagittarian women have itchy feet, and prefer all kinds of travel to sitting at home. They are not particularly good housewives – to be frank, cooking and cleaning is simply not for them. Their loved ones must learn to adapt to them, but Sagittarians themselves hate any pressure. They are not easy for men to handle, as Sagittarians want to be in charge. Sagittarius falls in love easily, is very sexual and temperamental, and may marry multiple times. Despite outward appearances, Sagittarius is a very lonely sign. Even after she is married with children, she may continue living as if she were alone; you might say she marches to the beat of her own drum. Younger

Sagittarians can be reckless, but as they mature, they can be drawn to religion, philosophy, and the occult.

Aries and Leo make the best matches, as Sagittarius is able to bend to Leo's ways, or at least pretend to. Sagittarians often end up with Aquarians, but their marriages do not tend to be for the long haul. They are attracted to Geminis, but are unlikely to marry one until middle age, when both signs have settled down. Sagittarius and Cancer have incredible sexual chemistry, but an actual relationship between them would be tumultuous and difficult. Capricorn can make a good partner- as long as they are able to respect each other's quirks. Sagittarius rarely ends up with a Virgo, and while she may often meet Pisces, things are unlikely to go very far.

CAPRICORN

Capricorn women are conscientious, reliable, organized, and hard-working. Many believe that life means nothing but work, and live accordingly. They are practical, and not particularly drawn to parties or loud groups of people. But if someone useful will be there, they are sure to make an appearance. Capricorn women are stingy, but not as much as their male counterparts. They are critical of others, but think highly of themselves. Generally, they take a difficult path in life, but thanks to their dedication, perseverance, and willingness to push their own limits, they are able to forge their own path, and by 45 or 50, they can provide themselves with anything they could want. Capricorn women have the peculiarity of looking older than their peers when they are young, and younger than everyone else once they have matured. They are not particularly sexual, and tend to be faithful partners. They rarely divorce, and even will fight until the end, even for a failed marriage. Many Capricorns have a pessimistic outlook of life, and have a tendency to be depressed. They are rarely at the center of any social circle, but are excellent organizers. They have a very rigid view of life and love, and are not interested in a fling, as marriage is the end goal. As a wife, Capricorn is simultaneously difficult and reliable. She is difficult because of her strict nature and difficulty adapting. But she will also take on all the household duties, and her husband can relax, knowing his children are in good hands.

Taurus, Pisces, and Scorpio make good matches. Aries is difficult, once things cool off after the initial honeymoon. When a Capricorn meets another Capricorn, they will be each other's first and last love. Sagittarius isn't a bad match, but they don't always pass the test of time. Aquarius and Capricorn are a difficult match, and rarely found together. Things are too dull with a Virgo, and while Leo can be exciting at first, things will fall apart when he begins showing off. Libra and Aquarius are both difficult partners for Capricorn, and she is rarely found with either of them.

AQUARIUS

A female Aquarius is very different from her male counterparts. She is calm and keeps a cool head, but she is also affectionate and open. She values loyalty above all else, and is unlikely to recover from any infidelity, though she will only divorce if this becomes a chronic trend, and she has truly been stabbed in the back. She is not interested in her partner's money, but rather, his professional success. She is unobtrusive and trusting, and will refrain from listening in on her partner's phone conversations or hacking into his email. With rare exceptions, Aquarian women make terrible housewives. But they are excellent partners in life – they are faithful, never boring, and will not reject a man, even in the most difficult circumstances. Most Aquarians are highly intuitive, and can easily tell the truth from a lie. They themselves only lie in extreme situations, which call for a "white lie" in order to avoid hurting someone's feelings.

Aquarius gets along well with Aries, Gemini, and Libra. She can also have a good relationship with a Sagittarius. Taurus often makes a successful match, though they are emotionally very different; the same goes for Virgo. Aquarius and Scorpio, Capricorn, or Cancer is a difficult match. Pisces can make a good partner as well, as both signs complement each other. Any relationship with a Leo will be tumultuous, but lasting, as Leo is selfish, and Aquarius will therefore have to be very forgiving.

PISCES

Pisces women are very adaptable, musically inclined, and erotic. They possess an innate earthly wisdom, and a good business sense. Pisces often reinvent themselves; they can be emotional, soft, and obstinate, as well as sentimental, at times. Their behavioral changes can be explained by frequent ups and downs. Pisces is charming, caring, and her outward malleability is very attractive to men. She is capable of loving selflessly, as long as the man has something to love. Even if he doesn't, she will try and take care of him until the very end. Pisces' greatest fear is poverty. They are intuitive, vulnerable, and always try to avoid conflict. They love to embellish the truth, and sometimes alcohol helps with this. Rarely, one finds extremely unbalanced, neurotic and dishonest Pisces, who are capable of turning their loved ones' lives into a living Hell!

Taurus, Capricorn, Cancer, and Scorpio make the best matches. She will be greatly attracted to a Virgo, but a lasting relationship is only likely if both partners are highly spiritual. Any union with a Libra is likely to be difficult and full of conflict. Pisces finds Gemini attractive, and they may have a very lively relationship – for a while. Occasionally, Pisces ends up with a Sagittarius, but she will have to fade into the background and entirely submit to him. If she ends up with an Aquarius, expect strong emotional outbursts, and a marriage that revolves around the need to raise their children.

Tatiana Borsch

Printed in Great Britain
by Amazon

68447095R00061